Ulster American

David Ireland

T0228714

methuen | drama

LONDON • NEW YORK • OXFORD • NEW DELHI • SYDNEY

METHUEN DRAMA
Bloomsbury Publishing Plc
50 Bedford Square, London, WC1B 3DP, UK
1385 Broadway, New York, NY 10018, USA
29 Earlsfort Terrace, Dublin 2, Ireland

BLOOMSBURY, METHUEN DRAMA and the Methuen
Drama logo are trademarks of Bloomsbury Publishing Plc

First published in Great Britain 2023

Cover design: Émilie Chen

Cover photo: Charlie Clift

A catalogue record for this book is available from the British Library.

A catalog record for this book is available from the Library of Congress.

ISBN: PB: 978-1-3504-6373-8
ePDF: 978-1-3504-6375-2
eBook: 978-1-3504-6374-5

Series: Modern Plays

Typeset by Mark Heslington Ltd, Scarborough, North Yorkshire

To find out more about our authors and books visit
www.bloomsbury.com and sign up for our newsletters.

ULSTER AMERICAN
by David Ireland

Cast

Jay Conway	**Woody Harrelson**
Leigh Carver	**Andy Serkis**
Ruth Davenport	**Louisa Harland**
Understudy for Leigh and Jay	**Mat Betteridge**
Understudy for Ruth	**Aoife Boyle**

Creative Team

Writer	**David Ireland**
Director	**Jeremy Herrin**
Set & Costume Designer	**Max Jones**
Lighting Designer	**Oliver Fenwick**
Sound Designer	**Emma Laxton**
Fight Director	**Renny Krupinski**
Casting Director	**Jessica Ronane CDG**
Associate Director	**Nicky Allpress**
Costume Supervisor	**Sabia Smith**
Props Supervisor	**Kate Margretts**
Voice & Dialect Coach	**Hazel Holder**
Production Manager	**Juli Fraire**
Marketing Director	**Stacy Coyne Wright**
Press and PR	**Bread and Butter PR**

Second Half Productions

Co-Founders & Directors	**Jeremy Herrin**
	Alan Stacey
	Rob O'Rahilly
Casting Director	**Jessica Ronane**
Creative Associate	**Lucie Lovatt**
Associate Producer & General Manager	**Alecia Marshall**
Production Coordinator	**Grace Nelder**
Production Assistant	**Immie Maclean**
Finance Manager	**Sophie Wells**
Casting Associate	**Abby Galvin**
Casting Assistant	**Poppy Apter**

SECOND
HALF
PRODUCTIONS

Ulster American was first produced and performed 3 August 2018 at the Traverse Theatre, Scotland, with the following cast and creatives:

Cast

Jay Conway — **Darrell D'Silva**
Leigh Carver — **Robert Jack**
Ruth Davenport — **Lucianne McEvoy**

Creative Team

Writer — **David Ireland**
Director — **Gareth Nicholls**
Designer — **Becky Minto**
Lighting Designer — **Kate Bonney**
Composer & Sound Designer — **Michael John McCarthy**
Fight Director — **EmmaClaire Brightlyn**
Assistant Director — **Kolbrún Björt Sigfúsdóttir**

Production Team

Production Manager — **Kevin McCallum**
Chief Electrician — **Renny Robertson**
Deputy Electrician — **Claire Elliot**
Head of Stage — **Gary Staerck**
Lighting & Sound Technician — **Tom Saunders**
Company Stage Manager — **Gemma Turner**
Deputy Stage Manager — **Judy Stewart**
Assistant Stage Manager — **Jessica Ward**
Costume Supervisor — **Sophie Ferguson**

Woody Harrelson
Jay Conway

Woody Harrelson's rare mix of intensity and charisma consistently surprises and delights audiences and critics alike in both mainstream and independent projects. Most recently Harrelson's performance in Martin McDonagh's, *Three Billboards Outside Ebbing, Missouri* earned him a 2018 Academy Award® nomination for Best Supporting Actor and a BAFTA nomination for Best Actor in a Supporting Role. He was previously nominated by the Academy, the Golden Globes® and SAG Awards® in the category of Best Actor for his portrayal of controversial magazine publisher Larry Flynt in Milos Forman's *The People vs. Larry Flynt*. His portrayal of a casualty notification officer in Oren Moverman's *The Messenger* garnered him a 2010 Academy Award® nomination for Best Supporting Actor.

Harrelson next joins Scarlett Johansson and Channing Tatum in the Greg Berlanti-directed film *Project Artemis* for Apple Original Films, set around the 1960s space race. Harrelson recently completed shooting *Suncoast* alongside Laura Linney, a drama written and directed by Laura Chinn in her directorial debut for Searchlight Films.

Harrelson recently starred opposite Justin Theroux in *The White House Plumbers*, a five-part limited series for HBO Max. Harrelson starred in Bobby Farrelly's sports comedy for Focus Features, *Champions*, based on the Goya Award winning Spanish film *Campeones*. Harrelson can be seen in Ruben Ostlund's English language ensemble film *Triangle of Sadness* which made its world debut at the 2022 Cannes Film Festival where it received an eight-minute standing ovation and won the Palme D'Or.

Other recent film credits include Columbia Pictures' action-comedy *The Man from Toronto* starring opposite Kevin Hart; Sony Picture's *Venom: Let There Be Carnage* as Cletus Kasady opposite supervillain 'Carnage' played by Tom Hardy; Netflix's *The Highwaymen* with Kevin Costner and Kathy Bates; *Midway* opposite Mandy Moore; Lucasfilm's *Solo: A Star Wars Story*, *Shock and Awe* and *LBJ* both directed by Rob Reiner; *The Glass Castle* co-starring Naomi Watts; the third installment of the *Planet of The Apes*, entitled *War for the Planet of the Apes* directed by Matt Reeves; Fox Searchlight's critically acclaimed *The Edge of Seventeen*; *Wilson* with director Craig Johnson; *Now You*

See Me 2 for director Jon Chu; and *Triple Nine* for director John Hillcoat.

Harrelson wrote, directed, produced and starred in an unprecedented live feature film *Lost in London*, which was broadcast live into theatres nationwide on 19 January 2017. The comedy also starred Owen Wilson and Willie Nelson.

Other highlights from Harrelson's film career include *Rampart* with director Oren Moverman; Ruben Fleischer's box office hit, *Zombieland* as well as the 2019 sequel *Zombieland: Double Tap*; *Out of the Furnace* starring opposite Christian Bale and Casey Affleck; *The Hunger Games* film series; *Now You See Me*; *The Grand*; *No Country for Old Men; A Scanner Darkly*; *A Prairie Home Companion*; *Seven Pounds*; *The Prize Winner of Defiance, Ohio*; *North Country*; *Transsiberian*; *The Thin Red Line*; *Welcome to Sarajevo*; *Natural Born Killers; Indecent Proposal*; *White Men Can't Jump* and was recently seen as the on screen host for director Pete McGrain's powerful political documentary *Ethos*.

On television, Harrelson most recently reprised his role as 'Archie Bunker' in two episodes of the Critics' Choice and Emmy-winning ABC special *Live in Front of a Studio Audience*, produced by Jimmy Kimmel and Norman Lear.

Other notable television credits include HBO's *True Detective* co-starring Matthew McConaughey for which he was nominated for Emmy and SAG Awards in the lead actor category and a Golden Globes Award for lead actor in a Mini Series. In 2012 Harrelson starred opposite Julianne Moore and Ed Harris in the HBO film *Game Change* for which he earned Primetime Emmy®, SAG Awards®, and Golden Globe® nominations for his role as Steve Schmidt, and Martin McDonagh's *Seven Psychopaths*, alongside Sam Rockwell, Colin Farrell and Christopher Walken.

Harrelson first endeared himself to millions of viewers as a member of the ensemble cast of NBC's long-running hit comedy, *Cheers*. For his work as the affable bartender 'Woody Boyd,' he won a Primetime Emmy® in 1988 and was nominated four additional times during his eight-year run on the show. In 1999, he gained another Primetime Emmy® nomination when he reprised the role in a guest appearance on the spin-off series *Frasier*.

Balancing his film and television work, in 1999 Harrelson directed his own play, *Furthest from the Sun* at the Theatre de la Juene Lune in

Minneapolis. He followed next with the Roundabout's Broadway revival of *The Rainmaker*; Sam Shepard's *The Late Henry Moss*, and John Kolvenbach's *On an Average Day* opposite Kyle MacLachlan in London's West End. Harrelson directed the Toronto premiere of Kenneth Lonergan's *This Is Our Youth* at Toronto's Berkeley Street Theatre. In the winter of 2005 Harrelson returned to London's West End, starring in Tennessee Williams' *Night of the Iguana* at the Lyric Theatre. In 2011, Harrelson co-wrote and directed the semi-autobiographical comedy *Bullet for Adolf* at Hart House Theatre in Toronto. In the summer of 2012 *Bullet for Adolf* made its Off-Broadway debut at New World Stages.

Andy Serkis
Leigh Carver

Andy Serkis is an award-winning actor who has earned acclaim from both critics and audiences for his work in a range of memorable roles. He gained legions of fans around the globe for his performance as 'Gollum' in the Academy Award®-winning *The Lord of the Rings* trilogy, directed by Peter Jackson. Serkis won an Empire Award for his role, in addition to sharing in several Outstanding Ensemble Cast Awards, including a Screen Actors Guild Award®. He reunited with Jackson in the director's epic retelling of *King Kong*, taking performance capture to another level as the titular character, and between 2011–2017 he took performance capture to new heights with his heartbreaking and critically acclaimed portrayal of 'Caesar' in the *Planet of the Apes* trilogy.

Serkis is currently in production as director/producer of an animated adaptation of George Orwell's *Animal Farm*.

In February of 2020, he was honoured by the British Academy of Film and Television Arts (BAFTA) at the 73rd EE British Academy Film Awards with one the organization's highest honour, the Outstanding British Contribution to Cinema Award.

Most recently, Serkis appeared in the feature film *Luther: The Fallen Sun,* starring alongside Idris Elba and Cynthia Erivo for Netflix and the BBC. In the fall of 2022, he received critical acclaim from press and fans for his portrayal of 'Kino Loy' in a three-episode arc of *Andor*, starring opposite Diego Luna. Additionally, he helmed *Venom: Let There Be Carnage* for Marvel and Sony Pictures and starred alongside Robert Pattinson in *The Batman,* portraying 'Alfred Pennyworth'.

Louisa Harland

Ruth Davenport

Before commencing her training at Mountview, Louisa appeared as a series regular in *Love/Hate* for RTE alongside Aidan Gillen and Robert Sheehan. Further screen credits include Channel 5's *The Deceived*; Discovery's mini-series *Harley and the Davidsons*; Woody Harrelson's feature film *Lost in London*; and Jack Rooke's award winning comedy *Big Boys*. In 2022, the third and final season of *Derry Girls*, aired to wide-spread critical acclaim.

On stage Louisa starred in the one woman show *Cotton Fingers* with National Theatre Wales and performed in a sell-out run at the Royal Court of *Glass. Kill. Bluebeard. Imp*; a collection of new plays by Caryl Churchill. Most recently she starred as Agnes in *Dancing at Lughnasa* at the National Theatre directed by Josie Rourke.

Louisa played a leading role alongside Jack Rowan in the comedy/horror feature film *Boys From County Hell*, and she has recently wrapped *Joy* directed by Ben Taylor, where she features alongside Bill Nighy and James Norton.

Louisa will be playing the title role in Sally Wainwright's highly-anticipated new Disney+ series, *The Ballad of Renegade Nell*, and early next year she will join Brian Cox and Patricia Clarkson on stage in *Long Day's Journey Into Night* directed by Jeremy Herrin.

David Ireland
Writer

David Ireland is a writer and actor from Belfast. He won the Meyer Whitworth Award in 2012 for *Everything Between Us* and was shortlisted for the Evening Standard Award for Most Promising Playwright 2016 for *Cyprus Avenue*. *Cyprus Avenue* also won the Irish Times Award for Best New Play and the James Tait Black Award in 2017. In 2018, *Ulster American* won a Scotsman Fringe First and the Critics Award for Theatre in Scotland for Best New Play. His other plays include *Not Now, Sadie, Yes So I Said Yes*, *The End of Hope* and *Can't Forget About You*.

He has written several radio plays and, for television, an episode of *The Young Offenders* (RTE/BBC).

His six-part romantic comedy series *The Lovers* was broadcast on Sky Atlantic earlier this year.

He is currently working on new plays for the Almeida, the National Theatre of Scotland and Paines Plough and a new television series for ITV and Sister Pictures.

As an actor he is best known for playing Clare's dad in *Derry Girls*. He has also appeared in *Shetland*, *Still Game*, *Taggart* and *The Lovers*.

Jeremy Herrin
Director

Jermey Herrin trained as a theatre director at both the National Theatre and the Royal Court, where he became Deputy Artistic Director in 2008. Between 2000 and 2008 he was an Associate Director at Live Theatre in Newcastle upon Tyne. Jeremy replaced Rupert Goold as Artistic Director of Headlong Theatre in September 2013. In 2007, he directed the UK premiere of David Hare's play, *The Vertical Hour*, as well as Polly Stenham's award-winning *That Face* at the Royal Court. *That Face* later transferred to London's West End, where it starred Lindsay Duncan and Matt Smith and was produced by Sonia Friedman. Two years later, in 2009, Jeremy directed Polly's second play, *Tusk Tusk* for which he was nominated for an Evening Standard Best Director Award. Other work at the Royal Court includes EV Crowe's *Hero*, Richard Bean's *The Heretic*, *Kin*, *Spur of the*

Moment, Off The Endz and *The Priory*, which won an Olivier Award for best Comedy.

In 2012 Jeremy directed the Olivier-nominated *This House*, written by James Graham, at the National Theatre. The production was revived at the Garrick Theatre at the end of 2016 and toured the UK in 2018.

In 2014 Jeremy directed the critically acclaimed adaptations of Hilary Mantel's novels *Wolf Hall* and *Bring up the Bodies* for the RSC and was nominated for an Olivier Award for Best Director. The productions transferred to the West End at the end of 2014 and opened on Broadway in April 2015. He also directed the Broadway production of *Noises Off* which opened in January 2016. His production of *People, Places and Things* at the National Theatre transferred to the Wyndham's Theatre in March 2016 and then to St Ann's Warehouse in October 2017. Jeremy directed James Graham's Oliver Award Winning *Labour of Love* which opened in November 2017 and his production of David Hare's *The Moderate Soprano* transferred from Hampstead Theatre to the West End in April 2018.

Jeremy directed *Noises Off* at the Garrick Theatre, *The Visit* at the National Theatre and *After Life* at the National Theatre and *The Mirror and The Light* at the Gielgud, West End, and *The Glass Menagerie* at the Duke of York's Theatre. For TV Jeremy directed *Talking Heads* and *Unprecedented* for the BBC.

Jeremy has most recently directed the world premiere of *A Mirror* at the Almeida Theatre starring Johnny Lee Miller, Tanya Reynolds and Micheal Ward, and the West End production of *Best of Enemies* starring Zachary Quinto and David Harewood at the Noël Coward Theatre.

Max Jones
Set & Costumer Designer

Max Jones is a London based, Bristol-born stage designer who graduated from The Royal Welsh College of Music and Drama in 2001. He is a winner of The Linbury Biennial Prize for Stage Design, and has since continued to design production, sets and costumes for live performance across the UK and internationally. Max was an Associate Artist at Clwyd Theatr Cymru between 2008–2015.

Most recent and forthcoming productions include: *A Mirror* (Almeida Theatre) by Sam Holcroft; *The Inquiry* (Chichester Festival Theatre) by

Harry Davies; *Anna Karenina* (Theatre Cocoon, Tokyo), adapted by Phillip Breen; *Jekyll and Hyde* (Reading Rep) by Gary McNair; *The Comedy of Errors* (RSC) by William Shakespeare; *Long Day's Journey into Night* (Theatre Cocoon, Tokyo) by Eugene O'Neill; *All My Sons* (Old Vic/Headlong and NT Live) by Arthur Miller; *Noises Off* by Michael Frayn (Lyric Hammersmith and West End); *Sydney and the Old Girl* (Park Theatre) by Eugene O'Hare; *Crime and Punishment* adapted by Phillip Breen (Theatre Cocoon, Tokyo); *Love and Information* by Caryl Churchill (Sheffield Crucible Theatre); *Shakespeare in Love* adapted by Lee Hall (UK tour); *A Streetcar Named Desire* by Tennessee Williams (Theatre Cocoon, Tokyo); *The House They Grew Up In* by Deborah Bruce (Chichester Festival Theatre/Headlong); *The Hypocrite* by Richard Bean (Hull Truck/RSC as part of Hull City of Culture 2017); *Trainspotting* by Irvine Welsh (Glasgow Citizens Theatre); *Pride and Prejudice* by Jane Austen (Regent's Park Open Air Theatre and tour); *The Mystery Plays* (York Minster); *The Crucible* by Arthur Miller (Manchester Royal Exchange); *Orpheus Descending* by Tennessee Williams (Theatre Cocoon, Tokyo); *Little Shop of Horrors* (Clwyd Theatr Cymru) and *The Broken Heart* by John Ford (Globe Theatre).

Oliver Fenwick
Lighting Designer

Theatre credits include: *The Father and the Assassin, Kerry Jackson, Blues for an Alabama Sky, Tartuffe, Ugly Lies the Bone, The Motherf***er with the a Hat, The Great Wave, The Holy Rosenburgs* (National Theatre); *Clyde's, Trouble in Butetown, Sweat, The Vote, One Night in Miami, Berenice* (Donmar Warehouse); *The Magician's Elephant, Wendy and Peter Pan, The Jew of Malta, Much Ado About Nothing, Love's Labour's Lost, The Winter's Tale, The Taming of the Shrew, Julius Caesar, The Grain Store, The Drunks* (RSC); *The Best Exotic Marigold Hotel* (UK tour); *Girls and Boys, Lela and Co, Routes, The Witness* (The Royal Court); *Handbagged, The Invisible Hand, Pass Over, When the Crows Visit, White Teeth, Holy Sh!t, Multitudes, The Colby Sisters, A Boy and His Soul, Bracken Moor, Red Velvet* (also St Ann's, NY), *Paper Dolls* (Kiln Theatre); *Oleanna* (Arts Theatre); *The Yeoman of the Guard* (ENO); *Carmen* (WNO); *The Sun, the Moon and the Stars, Noye's Fludde* (Theatre Royal Stratford); *Cabaret* (Gothenburg Opera); *Hansel and Gretel, To Kill a Mockingbird, Hobson's Choice* (Regent's Park); *Admissions* (Trafalgar Studios); *The Merry Widow* (Opera North); *Calendar Girls* (UK tour); *Genesis Inc., Mother Christmas, Gloria, Occupational Hazards, Reasons to be*

Happy (Hampstead Theatre); *Looking at Lucien, Thérèse Raquin, The Big Meal, King Lear, Candida, The Madness of King George III* (Theatre Royal Bath); *The Merchant of Venice* (New York, Washington, Chicago, China); *King Lear, The King's Speech* (Chichester); *King Lear, Bakersfield Mist, Handbagged, The Madness of King George III, The Importance of Being Earnest, Ghosts* (West End); *Private Lives, Blue Orange* (UK tour); *Right Now* (also Bush, Traverse); *Travels with my Aunt* (Menier Chocolate Factory); *After Miss Julie* (Young Vic); A Midsummer Night's Dream (Lyric, Hammersmith); *Pride and Prejudice, The Comedy of Errors* (Sheffield); *Into the Woods, Sunday in the Park with George* (Chatelet, Paris); *Les Miserables* (Jonkoping/Wermland, Sweden); *Romeo and Juliet* (Tokyo, Japan).

Emma Laxton
Sound Designer

Emma trained at the Central School of Speech and Drama. She was the Deputy Head of Sound at the Royal Court from 2002–2007. She has also worked as a senior sound technician in the Olivier at the National Theatre.

Emma won an Olivier Award for Best Sound Design for *Emilia* in 2020 and the Falstaff Award for Best Sound Design/Original Score for her work on *Coriolanus* at the Donmar Warehouse in 2014.

Recent theatre credits include: *Mlima's Tale* (Kiln); *Dancing at Lughnasa* (National Theatre); *The Collaboration, Hamlet, Blood Wedding, See Me Now* (Young Vic); *Walden* (Harold Pinter Theatre, West End); *A Kind of People, Superhoe, The Living Newspaper: Edition 1* (Royal Court); *The Effect, Julius Caesar, Sisters, Coriolanus* (Sheffield Theatres); *Vassa, The Writer* (Almeida); *Emilia* (West End); *The Country Wife, Random/Generations, The House They Grew Up In, Forty Years On* (Chichester Festival Theatre); *Titus Andronicus* (RSC and Barbican Centre); *Trouble in Butetown, The York Realist, Limehouse, Measure for Measure, Coriolanus, Berenice, The Physicists, Making Noise Quietly, The Recruiting Officer* (Donmar Warehouse); *Breaking the Code, All My Sons, A Doll's House, Three Birds, The Accrington Pals, Lady Windermere's Fan* (Royal Exchange, Manchester); *Sweet Charity* (Nottingham Playhouse); *Ghosts, The Oresteia* (Home Theatre, Manchester); *Observe the Sons of Ulster Marching Towards the Somme* (Headlong, UK tour); *Great Expectations* (West Yorkshire Playhouse); *Elizabeth* (Royal Opera House); *101 Dalmations, The Lion, the Witch and the Wardrobe*

(Birmingham Rep); *Henry the Fifth* (Unicorn Theatre, Imaginate Festival); *All My Sons* (Talawa Theatre, UK tour); *Uncle Vanya, Hello/ Goodbye, The Blackest Black, #Aiww: The Arrest of Ai Wei Wei, Lay Down Your Cross, Blue Heart Afternoon* (Hampstead Theatre); *Cat On A Hot Tin Roof* (Royal Exchange/ Royal & Derngate/Northern Stage); *Pests* (Clean Break/Royal Exchange/Royal Court); *Much Ado About Nothing* (Old Vic); *Nut, Men Should Weep, Shoot/Get Treasure/ Repeat* (National Theatre); *Omg!* (Sadler's Wells/The Place/Company of Angels); *There Are Mountains* (Clean Break/HMP Askham Grange); *The Promise* (Donmar Warehouse at Trafalgar Studios); *You Can Still Make a Killing* (Southwark Playhouse); *The Sacred Flame* (ETT); *Black T-Shirt Collection* (Fuel UK tour and National Theatre); *Invisible* (Transport UK tour and Luxemborg); *Much Ado About Nothing* (Wyndham's Theatre, West End); *Precious Little Talent* (Trafalgar Studios), *Where's My Seat, Like a Fishbone, The Whiskey Taster, If There Is I Haven't Found It Yet, 2nd May 1997, Apologia, The Contingency Plan, Wrecks, Broken Space Season, 2000 Feet Away* (Bush Theatre); *Charged* (Clean Break/Soho Theatre); *My Romantic History* (Sheffield Theatres/Bush Theatre); *Travels With My Aunt* (Northampton Theatre Royal); *Pornography* (Birmingham Rep/ Traverse/Tricycle Theatre); *Europe* (Dundee Rep/Barbican Pit).

Renny Krupinski
Fight Director

Renny is an internationally renowned fight director, award-winning actor, director and writer.

Theatre fight work includes: London's West End, The RSC, National Theatre, Shakespeare's Globe, Young Vic, National Theatre of Scotland, Glasgow Citz, Manchester Royal Exchange, Theatr Clwyd, Crucible Sheffield to name but a few.

TV fights include: *Emmerdale* (social media accolade of 'Best punch ever'), *Coronation Street, Hollyoaks, Blue Murder, Man Like Mobeen, Jamaica Inn, So Awkward* series 1–8, *So Awkward Kids Club, Goldies Oldies, A Kind of Spark*, the multi-award-winning film *Tyrannosaur* and *The Latent Image*, released earlier this year. He was stunt co-ordinator for the BBC series *Dodger* and for series 12 and 13 of *Death in Paradise*.

As an actor he has played, among others, Salieri (twice), Banquo, Claudius, Capulet, Launcelot Gobbo and the villain Sizzler In

Brookside. Most recently he filmed the role of Dr Gower in *The Tower* series 2, Harry Pettifer in *Miss Scarlet and the Duke* series 4, Lubos Sterba in *Grace* series 4 and Joe in the romantic comedy *Upgraded*, all for release next year.

As a writer his play *D'Eon* was a 5* critically acclaimed sell-out at Hope Mill Theatre Manchester, was translated into Greek and ran for three months in Athens. Renny has written many BBC Radio 4 comedies, was a regular writer for *The Bill* and won a Scotsman Fringe First in Edinburgh for his play Bare.

Renny is the voice and face of Oblivion at Alton Towers. Recently he has directed the fights for the current national tour of *And Then There Were None*, The RSC's ground-breaking production of *The Comedy of Errors*, *Much Ado About Nothing* at Shakespeare's Globe, *Zorro the Musical* and *From Here to Eternity* at The Charing Cross Theatre.

Jessica Ronane CDG
Casting Director

Jessica Ronane's recent theatre credits include: *A Mirror* (Almeida Theatre); *The Lehman Trilogy* (Gillian Lynne Theatre) and *The Glass Menagerie* (Duke of York's Theatre).

Her work at The Old Vic includes: *Pygmalion*, *The Dumb Waiter*, *Faith Healer*, *Camp Siegfried*, *Endgame/Rough for Theatre II*, *A Christmas Carol*, *Lungs*, *A Very Expensive Poison*, *Present Laughter*, *All My Sons*, *The American Clock*, *SYLVIA*, *A Monster Calls*, *Mood Music*, *Fanny & Alexander*, *Woyzeck*, *Rosencrantz & Guildenstern Are Dead*, *King Lear*, *The Caretaker*, *The Master Builder*, *Dr. Seuss's The Lorax*, *The Hairy Ape*, *Future Conditional*, *Girl from the North Country* (The Old Vic/West End) and *The Divide* (The Old Vic/ EIF).

Upcoming theatre work includes: *Long Day's Journey Into Night* (Wyndham's Theatre).

Jessica Ronane's film credits include: *Mickey 17* (Bong Joon Ho); *Queer* (Luca Guadagnino); *Good Grief* (Dan Levy); *Emma* (Autumn de Wilde) and *The Kid Who Would Be King* (Joe Cornish). Upcoming films include *Parliament Square* and *Julie* both to be directed by Josie Rourke.

Television credits include: *True Detective: Night Country* and *The Amazing Mr. Blunden*.

Jessica is Casting Director for Second Half Productions and Casting Consultant for The Old Vic.

Sabia Smith
Costume Supervisor

Sabia Smith studied Costume Construction and Supervision at The Royal Academy of Dramatic Art.

Theatre and opera credits include: *Next to Normal*, *Love and Other Acts of Violence* (Donmar Warehouse); *Robin Hood* (Regent's Park); *The Duchess of Malfi*, *A Midsummer Night's Dream*, *Hakawatis*, *Midsummer Mechanicals* (Shakespeare's Globe); *The Inquiry* (Chichester Festival Theatre); *The Marriage of Figaro* (Royal Academy of Music); *Message in a Bottle* (Sadler's Wells and Universal Music); *God's of the Game: A Football Opera*, *La Gioconda*, *The Life and Death of Alexander Litvinenko*, *Falstaff*, *Don Carlos* (Grange Park Opera); *Favour* (Bush Theatre); *The Marriage of Figaro* (The Royal Academy of Music); *Anne of Green Gables* (London Children's Ballet); *The Magic Flute* (The Royal College of Music); *Noises Off* (Playful Productions and the Lyric Hammersmith); *WhoDunnit [Unrehearsed]* (Park Theatre); *Zauberland* (Theatres des Bouffes du Nord; The Royal Opera House; La Monnaie/De Munt, Bruxelles; Opéra de Lille; The Lincoln Center for the Performing Arts; Opéra de Rouen Normandie); *The American Clock* (Old Vic); *Twelfth Night* (Watermill Theatre and Wilton's Music Hall); *We're Stuck!* (China Plate and Shoreditch Town Hall).

TV and film credits include: *Gods of the Game: A Football Opera* (Sky Arts); *NewsHub* commercial and *Nation Down*.

Kate Margretts
Props Supervisor

Kate trained at the Liverpool Institute for Performing Arts (LIPA) in Theatre Performance Technology before starting her career in Stage Management. This encompassed a multitude of roles in the West End, across the UK, and internationally.

After developing a greater passion for props and painting, Kate moved to the English National Opera as Running Props Manager and Head of Armoury. After three years working on various operas, including *Drive & Live: La bohème* (Alexandra Palace) during the pandemic, Kate moved back into freelancing full-time.

Recent productions as prop supervisor include: *Vanya* (Duke of York's Theatre, London/Richmond Theatre); *Free Your Mind* (Aviva Studios,

Manchester International Festival); *Close Up: The Twiggy Musical* (Menier Chocolate Factory, London); *Assassins* (Chichester Festival Theatre); *Peter Rabbit: The Easter Adventure* (Histrionic Productions); *Good* (Harold Pinter Theatre, London); *Charlie and the Chocolate Factory* (Leeds Playhouse, UK tour); *Saw: The Experience* (London); Monopoly Lifesized (London); *The Twits* (Curve Theatre, Leicester/ Rose Theatre, Kingston/Hong Kong & UK tour); *Romeo & Juliet/ Richard III* (Shakespeare Rose Theatre, York).

Hazel Holder
Voice & Dialect Coach

Theatre includes: *To Kill a Mockingbird, 2.22, The Glass Menagerie, Cock, Constellations, Tina: The Tina Turner Musical, Get Up Stand Up, Death of a Salesman, Uncle Vanya, Caroline, or Change, Dreamgirls* (West End); *Blues for an Alabama Sky, Small Island, Trouble in Mind, Rockets and Blue Lights, Death of England: Delroy, Death of England, Nine Night, Angels in America, Barber Shop Chronicles, Les Blancs, Ma Rainey* (National Theatre); *Jitney* (Old Vic); *The Doll's House Part 2, Marys Seacole* (Donmar); *Pass Over* (Kiln); *Fairview, The Convert* (Young Vic); *ear for eye, Poet in Da Corner* (Royal Court).

Television includes: *The Anansi Boys*; *The Baby*; *Small Axe*; *The Power*; *In the Long Run.*

Film includes: *Drift*; *Aisha*; *The Silent Twins*; *Ear for Eye*; *Death on the Nile.*

SECOND HALF PRODUCTIONS

Second Half Productions is an entertainment company founded by Jeremy Herrin, Alan Stacey and Rob O'Rahilly in 2021 to generate innovative productions for stage and screen. By commissioning world leading artists to create new work and by breathing new life into classic stories, we invigorate audiences in London, the UK and beyond. Our ambition is to produce entertainment that engages the broadest range of people and in doing so creates meaningful opportunities for those who are currently underrepresented in the sector. We're a company of creatives, producers and general managers and we're driven and inspired by the artists that we work with. Recent productions include *The Glass Menagerie* at the Duke of York's Theatre, *Best of Enemies* at Noël Coward Theatre, *A Mirror* at Trafalgar Theatre and *Long Day's Journey Into Night* at Wyndham's Theatre.

Ulster American

Characters

Jay Conway, *m, 40s. American. Actor.*
Leigh Carver, *m, 40s. English. Director.*
Ruth Davenport, *f, 30s. Northern Irish. Playwright.*

London, present day.

Leigh Carver's *living room. It's Sunday evening, around 8pm.* **Jay** *and* **Leigh** *sit on a sofa.* **Jay** *drinks a cup of chamomile tea.* **Leigh** *drinks red wine.*

Jay Is there homophobia in Hollywood? Of course. And misogyny? How can we deny it? It's reflected in so much of our output. Narrative upon narrative centred around the *abuse* of women, the *violent* abuse of women. And racism? Only a fool could pretend otherwise. We've come a long way since Stepin Fetchit . . . fuck we've come a long way since *Poitier* but still . . .

Leigh No, I agree with what you're saying.

Jay You ever use the n word?

Leigh Mm?

Jay You ever use the n word?

Leigh The *n* word?

Jay Yeah.

Leigh The actual word?

Jay Yeah, the actu–, you need me to say it?

Leigh *No.*

They laugh.

Jay So have you?

Leigh *shakes his head no.*

Jay Never?

Leigh Not that I remember.

Jay So you may have? If you were drunk or –

Leigh Maybe as a teenager.

Jay Ohh

Leigh   But it's unlikely. My parents were old communists so
. . . it wouldn't have been . . .

Jay   I've *never* said it. I don't even like saying the phrase
'The N Word'. Even referencing it obliquely like this causes
me discomfort.

Leigh   I know what you mean.

Jay   But I do wonder if that's right. Are we abnegating our
responsibility to history by refusing to speak the word?
Maybe we have a responsibility as white people to say it as
much as possible. To take possession of the word. As our
ancestors once took possession of the people. Not my
ancestors obviously.

Leigh   Nor mine.

Jay   My ancestors were – uh.

Leigh   Yeah, mine were probably . . .

Jay   They were not slave-owners.

Leigh   No. Nor mine.

Jay   You ever see Ice Cube on *Real Time*?

Leigh   What's *Real Time*?

Jay   It's a talk show.

Leigh   I don't know the American talk shows.

Jay   One week Bill Maher said the n word.

Leigh   Who's Bill Maher?

Jay   He's the host of the show.

Leigh   And he's white?

Jay   Yes.

Leigh   Ohhhhh . . .

Jay In context it was not without irony, but it still proved controversial.

Leigh Course

Jay So the next week they had Ice Cube on as a guest, I know Cube, he's very honest, straight-talking . . .

Leigh He's a rapper, isn't he?

Jay And a great one. If he'd been murdered in the nineties he would be spoken about with the same reverence as Tupac and Biggie, Big Pun.

Leigh Mm.

Jay Big L. And of course Eazy E.

Leigh Yasss.

Jay Cube made the mistake of surviving. It says something about America that we prefer our iconic black artists to meet unnecessary, preferably violent, deaths.

Leigh It's a tragedy.

Jay So on the show he said that under no circumstances can the white man say the n word anymore. 'That's our word now,' he said.

Leigh Right . . .

Jay And the studio audience applauded.

Leigh You can see his point of view.

Jay Completely. But I also love what Baldwin said.

Leigh What did Baldwin say?

Jay Baldwin said that that word had nothing to do with the black race. That it was an invention of the white race and was placed upon black people without their consent.

Leigh Who could argue with that?

Jay   So as it's the white's man word, it's the white man who must look inside himself and ask himself why he invented that word, why he needed that word in his lexicon. It's a really good question.

Leigh   It is a good question. And what was his conclusion?

Jay   Baldwin's conclusion?

Leigh   Yeah.

Jay   I don't think he had one.

Leigh   Mmm.

Jay   But I think that was his point. That it was a question for the white race.

Leigh   But surely the point he's making is that it's precisely his responsibility.

Jay   Is it?

Leigh   As a white man.

Jay   As a *white* man?

Leigh   Yes, as a white man, he has to answer for his racist language.

Jay   Who?

Leigh   Baldwin.

Jay   Baldwin was black.

Leigh   Really?

Jay   Definitely.

Leigh   No.

Jay   I promise you.

Leigh   Alec Baldwin's black?

Jay   *Alec* Baldwin?

Leigh   He must be very light-skinned, you can't even tell.

Jay   Not talking about *Alec* Baldwin.

Leigh   Who are you talking about?

Jay   James Baldwin.

Leigh   Ohhh!

Jay *laughs*. **Leigh** *laughs*.

Leigh   Is he the youngest one? The one who was on *Big Brother*?

Jay   No, James Baldw – you never heard of James Baldwin?

Leigh   I don't know all the Baldwin brothers by name. Was he the one in *Sliver*?

Jay   No, James Baldwin was uh . . . an African-American author – prolific in the sixties. He wrote *Notes of a Native Son*.

Leigh   Oh . . . yeessss . . . God, I'm a –

Jay   He was also gay.

Leigh   Of course I know who you mean now. I am a complete . . . forgive me.

Jay   He's not as well-known as he should be. Perhaps because America – and the world – wasn't ready to hear his voice. It was presumptuous of me to assume you would have heard of him.

Leigh   I have heard of him, I should have . . . I'm a fucking idiot. Sorry.

Pause.

Jay   Am I talking too much?

Leigh   No.

Jay   I get like this when I'm nervous.

Leigh   You've no need to be nervous. What are you nervous about?

Jay   The journey.

Leigh   Just jump on the Victoria line and change at King's Cross.

Jay *looks confused.* **Leigh** *realises his mistake.*

Leigh   Oh you mean . . .?

Jay   I mean the spiri –

Leigh   The internal . . .

Jay   The process . . .

Leigh (*at the same time*)   The process.

He repeats it, pronouncing it the American way, like **Jay***:*

Leigh   Process, yes. Well everyone's nervous at this stage! The other actors, they'll be very intimidated by you.

Jay   I don't want them to be intimidated.

Leigh   They should be intimidated. Your character is intimidating.

Jay   OK . . . OK . . . good.

Leigh   I like to keep things very relaxed on the first day anyway.

Jay   I cannot wait to meet our writer!

Leigh   I don't understand why she's so late.

Jay   I really want her to like me.

Leigh   She loves you.

Jay   I love her name. 'Ruth Davenport.' It's so real. So Irish.

Leigh   Well, she is real. And she is Irish.

Jay   I connected so much with this play I can't tell you.

Leigh   You have told me.

Jay   These *words*.

Leigh   Words are everything.

Jay   The savagery. The visceral rhythm and savagery.

Leigh   That's exactly what I said to her. It's visceral. Poetic.

Jay   Savage.

Leigh   Relentless. And yet compassionate.

Jay   Only a woman could write with this kind of relentless compassion.

Leigh   She is a woman.

Jay   I love that she's a woman. To hear a woman tell this kind of story. And this important moment in history. When women's voices are crying out to be heard.

Leigh   I think it's true we need to do more for women. Create more opportunities.

Jay   Agreed.

Leigh   Etcetera.

Jay   Well fucking listen to them for once.

Leigh   Yep.

Jay   Allow *them* to be heard. Learn from our mistakes. This is where we're at as a culture.

Leigh   Historical materialism.

Jay   You ever heard of the Bechdel theory?

Leigh   I've heard of the Bechdel *test*.

Jay   It's this theory that for a work of art to be truly progressive, it must feature two women talking.

Leigh   Yes, I'm familiar with it.

Jay   About something that's really important.

Leigh   And about something other than a man.

Jay   What?

Leigh   It has to feature two women talking about something other than a man.

Jay   That's the Bechdel theory?

Leigh   The Bechdel test, yes.

Jay   And they have to talk about something feminist, right?

Leigh   No.

Jay   Yeah, a woman told me this, they have to talk about something women give a fuck about. Rights. Voting. Equality. *Pay*.

Leigh   I don't think – all those issues are important – but I don't think that's strictly speaking part of the Bechdel test.

Jay   Well, it fucking should be. Bechdel should have added that to his fucking test. If he really gave a fuck about women.

Leigh   Bechdel was a woman.

Jay   No, I don't think so.

Leigh   She was. Is.

Jay   A woman told me Bechdel was a man.

Leigh   I'm sure Bechdel's a woman.

Jay   You sure?

Leigh   Yes.

Jay   Really sure?

Leigh   I am in fact one hundred per cent positive Bechdel is a woman.

Jay   Well, there you go. Right?

Leigh   Right?

Jay   Bechdel was a woman.

Leigh   Bechdel *is* a woman.

Jay   So that's an example. Why should I, a man, dictate to Bechdel, a woman, what should or should not be part of her fucking theory? This is me, learning from my mistakes, learning to shut the fuck up.

Leigh   I suppose.

Jay   And that's what I'm saying, this is where we're at. Guys like me and you taking a back seat. Allowing the Ruth Davenports of the world to have their say. Fucking white heteronormative, privileged fucking uh . . . *cis* . . . motherfuckers like you and I who have to stand aside now. We have a moral responsibility to . . . I mean not *me*. Obviously. I'm Irish Catholic, so I can't . . .

Leigh   Of course.

Jay   I'm not part of that – the equation of –

Leigh   Neither am I.

Jay   I have an intersectional exemption. Am I white? It's undeniable. Am I heterosexual? Yes, completely. Am I trans? Well, I love my dick, so no. But I'm not part of this rampant elite the, who, –

Leigh   And I'm English so . . .

Jay   Exactly, you're English, so –

Leigh   So I'm sort of . . . not really part of –

Jay   Because we have no power. Do you have power?

Leigh   Well, I run a theatre.

Jay   But that's not power. Not real power.

Leigh   I suppose not.

Jay   And I'm just an actor.

Leigh   Sure.

Jay   Admittedly I have *some* power.

Leigh   Well, you have a power onstage. And onscreen.

Jay   I would classify that as charisma more than power.

Leigh   And you have won an Oscar.

Jay   That means nothing to me. I've never sought external validation.

Leigh   It's why you're so good.

Jay   I work my program. I talk to my sponsor on a daily basis. On a daily basis I pray, I meditate, I maintain my relationship with a power greater than myself.

Leigh   Nice.

Jay   I told you I'm in AA, right?

Leigh   You did, yes.

Jay   Did I tell you my sponsor is a priest?

Leigh   Yes.

Jay   Being open with trusted colleagues helps me maintain my sobriety.

Leigh   Sensible.

Jay   I distanced myself from God, when I was a kid. I come from a big Catholic family.

Leigh   You told me this.

Jay   I turned my back on the Church when I discovered acting. Acting became my religion.

Leigh   Yes, we talked about this last time we met. It's really really fascinating.

Jay   When everyone else had turned their backs on me, it was God, it was the Church, it was the Twelve Steps, it was Father Michael Mulcahy, that lifted me up.

Leigh   Very moving.

Jay   So now I . . . I'm just trying to be a better fucking person now, Leigh. A better Catholic. Treat people with respect, starting with myself. Honour my truth. The truth of who I am.

Leigh   If one can't live truthfully, how does one live at all?

Jay   It's what drew me to this script. The truth of it.

Leigh   Yes.

Jay   And the unremitting violence.

Leigh   I know what you mean.

Jay   What it says of the Irish. And who we are as a people historically.

Leigh   History is so important.

Jay   And where we're going.

Leigh   Where are we going? Where are the Irish going? These are all important questions. Particularly in the current climate.

Jay   These tumultuous times.

Leigh   The post-Brexit environment.

Jay   And the rise of women. The voices of Irish women. And all women everywhere. Which must be heard.

Leigh   True,

Jay   A woman from England, a British writer, forgive me but it's true . . .

Leigh   What?

Jay   A British writer could never have written a play like this.

Leigh   A play set in Northern Ireland?

Jay   A play of this kind of emotional intensity.

Leigh   Why not?

Jay   Because of how emotionally repressed the British are.

Leigh   I don't think that's –

Jay   It's a stereotype?

Leigh   It may have been true at one point. But these days the British are more open, more emotionally articulate. Particularly since the death of Diana.

Jay   Diana who?

Leigh   Princess Diana. The Princess of Wales.

Jay   Oh. Oh *Diana*. Riiiight.

Leigh   'Our dead princess.'

Jay   Yeah yeah.

Leigh   When she died, there was a sea change.

Jay   I get it now.

Leigh   *They* say.

Jay   Now she's someone I would loved to have met.

Leigh   Really?

Jay   Just to have a conversation with her. Find out what *she* thought. I bet no one ever really spoke to her. I think her whole problem was no one ever saw her as a real human being with real problems and real feelings. And clearly Charles, Prince Charles, *King* Charles, he never loved her. At least not in the way that a woman like that needed to be loved.

Leigh Charles had a very old-fashioned view of marriage, I suspect. Not untypical of the Windsors.

Jay He needed to love that woman like a . . . well, like a princess. Actually. Because that's what she was. She was a princess. Even if she was a . . .

Leigh Hmm.

Jay A waitress. Had she been born a waitress.

Leigh Yes, that is a very interesting remark. Very perceptive. And very very interesting.

Jay *sets his can down and leans forward.*

Jay Would you mind if I asked you a troubling question?

Leigh . . . No.

Jay May I?

Leigh Go ahead.

Jay Do you think there are any circumstances where it's morally acceptable to rape someone?

Pause. **Leigh** *furrows his brow. He clears his throat.*

Leigh . . . Sorry?

Jay Is it ever OK to rape someone? A woman?

Leigh No. No I wouldn't have . . . *thought* so, sorry, why are we talking about this?

Jay I made a picture with Paul Verhoeven once. You won't have seen it, no one's seen it, it was very early in my career but there was a scene in it, eventually got cut from the script but it was a great scene where my character had to, uh – he was being held hostage in a room full of women. And this terrorist, this evil son of a bitch, played in the eventual movie by Rutger Hauer, who is the sweetest man – well, he forced my character at gun point to select one of the women to rape. And if I refused, he would detonate a nuclear bomb in downtown Minneapolis. Eventually, my character chose . . . one of the hostages was his ex-wife . . . so he chose her. Which he naturally felt conflicted about. It was a terrific scene and it really took the story to a whole 'nother level but too many people at the studio, mainly women it has to be said, found it objectionable. And maybe they were right. Maybe it did cross a line. But it got me thinking cos I like to think about things, that's what draws me to stories, it's what drew me to this story – am I provoked? Does it make me think? Does it make me see the world in a new way?

Leigh   Right, right.

Jay   And it got me thinking. If I had to rape someone. Who would I rape?

Leigh   Right. But you wouldn't actually want do that to anyone, would you?

Jay   Of course not, Leigh. I'm a fucking feminist. How could I not be? I benefit from the patriarchy yet I am nonetheless demeaned by it.

Leigh   I actually am a feminist.

Jay   Diana.

Leigh   What?

Jay   I would rape Princess Diana. If I had to. At gunpoint.

Leigh . . . Uhm . . .

Jay   Think about it, it was her life's mission to empathise with the oppressed and the marginalised. Them. Out there. You know? *AIDS. Landmines. Africa.* If you raped Diana, it would have given her a deeper sympathy with the victims of sexual assault. She could have used it in her work. Some good could come from it. Now I'm not for one minute justifying violence against women. But if you did wish to justify it. It can be done. So?

Leigh   So?

Jay   Who would you rape? If you had to?

Leigh . . . Uh . . . No one.

Jay   No one?

Leigh   No one.

Jay   You can choose anyone in the world.

Leigh   I wouldn't.

Jay   But if someone put a gun to your head?

Leigh   I still wouldn't.

Jay   Right, but if someone put a gun to your head?

Leigh   Yes, I understand but I still wouldn't.

Jay   They're going to kill you.

Leigh   I understand.

Jay   They have a gun to your head.

Leigh   I know.

Jay   They'll detonate a nuclear bomb.

Leigh   I understand what you're, the premise of, but I – I wouldn't. They would have to kill me.

Jay   I don't think you understand.

Leigh   I do understand.

Jay   It's Rutger Hauer.

Leigh   Yes, I know, but – I just could never . . . under any . . . It's wrong.

A momentary pause.

Jay   What if it was Jesus?

Leigh   Sorry?

Jay   What if Jesus put a gun to your head?

Leigh   Well . . . I'm not a Christian but –

Jay   You don't have to be a Christian.

Leigh   I'm not a Christian but –

Jay   Yeah, you don't have to be a Christian.

Leigh   If you'll let me finish my *bloody* . . .!

Pause.

I'm not a Christian but from what I know of Jesus, from what I've read of his teachings, I don't think it would be in his character to put a gun to a person's head and request that they sexually assault someone.

A silence. **Jay** *seems to disappear into himself. The silence seems to go on forever.* **Jay** *won't look at* **Leigh**. **Leigh** *is unsure how to respond.*

Then . . .

Leigh   Thatcher.

Jay *looks up.*

Leigh   Margaret Thatcher. If I was forced to . . . 'do that' . . . to anyone. I would . . . Thatcher.

Jay   Why?

Leigh   Everything about that woman was . . . I grew up somewhere . . . well, everything that woman stood for disgusts me . . .

Jay   OK . . .

Leigh   But even she didn't deserve that. No one deserves that.

Pause.

Jay   Have I upset you?

Leigh   No.

Jay   Cos I'm sensing this uh, if you'll excuse me, this sense of passive resistance from you.

Leigh   From *me*?

Jay   This attitude of barely concealed resentment like I've said something to offend you?

Leigh   Not at all. I don't know where you're getting that from.

Jay   If I've offended you, you have to tell me. I know I can be overwhelming. I know I can be intense.

Leigh   You haven't offended me.

Jay   It would kill me to offend you. I know we've only known each other a short time but I feel that I can trust you with my life.

Leigh   You absolutely can.

Jay   There is no more important relationship, Leigh, than the relationship between an actor and a director. It's as important as the relationship between a mother and a new born.

Leigh   I honestly couldn't agree more.

Jay   For the next four weeks you are my mother. You are my father. You are my lover, my king, my cousin, my brother. My wife, my fuckbuddy, my cuck, my nemesis, my *dick*. That's the level of –

Leigh   Yes.

Jay   That I put you at.

Leigh   Well, I am humbled. And you have not offended me.

Jay   Great. OK. Great.

Leigh *gets up and heads for the kitchen.*

Leigh   Would you excuse me for a second?

Jay   Everything OK?

Leigh   I'm just going to uh, are you OK for drinks?

Jay   I'm fine. Thank you.

Leigh *enters the kitchen.* **Jay** *flicks through his script. He reads the lines to himself in a terrible Belfast accent.*

Jay   'You fucking dirty Fenian bastard. You fucking dirty Fenian fuck.'

He plays with the word in his mouth.

'Fenians.' 'Fenians.' 'Fenians.' 'I hate the Fenians.' 'I hate the Fenians.' 'I want to murder all the Fenians.'

Leigh *re-enters with a huge glass of wine.*

Jay   Do you think I could have an eyepatch?

Leigh   A what?

Jay   An eyepatch.

Leigh   You mean for the play?

Jay   I think it would be a great metaphor for my character's moral decay.

The buzzer goes. **Leigh** *goes to answer it.*

Jay   Is that Ruth?

Leigh   I hope so.

When **Leigh** *goes out to the hall,* **Jay** *stands up, makes a great fuss over himself. He fixes his hair, maybe does some star jumps. From the hall, we hear* **Leigh** *welcoming* **Ruth**.

Leigh (*from off*)   Hi!

Ruth (*from off*)   Hello!!! Hello!

Leigh (*from off*)   Come in come in!

Leigh *enters, followed by* **Ruth**.

Leigh Ruth this is, ah . . .

Jay Hi, Ruth. I'm Jay Conway.

Ruth Oh I know who you are! Hello! I'm Ruth . . . eh . . .
Davenport, hi.

She offers her hand and they shake.

It's really nice to meet you.

Jay It's so great to meet you.

Ruth I'm so sorry we haven't been able to meet before it's
just the dates and –

Jay Forget about it.

Leigh Is everything OK?

Ruth Yes, I'm sorry I'm so late.

Leigh What happened? Why didn't you call?

Ruth My phone ran out of battery. And God . . . so . . . I
was . . . my mother was driving me to the airport. And we've
been arguing a lot lately, really getting under each other's
skin, that's the kind of relationship we have and I love her
but she's really fucking . . . you know how it is with parents.

Leigh She's quite something, Ruth's mother. You'll meet
her.

Jay Can't wait!

Ruth So, we're bickering about everything and she asks
when I'm coming back from London and I tell her not for
another month or two and she says, 'Sure I'm going away to
Portrush with Joan Maginness next week, who's gonna feed
the cat?' And I'm like 'Get Kelly to do it', Kelly's my sister so
. . .

Jay You live with your mom?

Ruth Yeah yeah.

Leigh   Would you like a drink?

Ruth   No. Yes actually.

Leigh   Wine?

Ruth   Yeah. So I'm . . .

Leigh   Red OK?

Ruth   Yeah yeah.

Leigh *exits.*

Ruth   So she says, 'I can't ask Kelly, she's too busy with the kids' and I'm like 'Mum I've got a play opening in London with Jay Conway in it, I'm not coming back to Belfast to feed the cat'. But she's no idea who you are.

Jay   Oh!

Ruth   Sorry! She hasn't been to the cinema since *Dr Zhivago*, so –

Jay   Great movie.

Ruth   Then she says, 'This isn't another play about the Troubles, is it? People are sick of hearing about the Troubles!'

Leigh *re-enters, handing a glass of wine to* **Ruth**.

Leigh   There you go.

Ruth   Thanks. Then she says, 'You're too young to remember the Troubles, anyway'. And I'm like 'Mummy I grew up in the nineties of course I remember the Troubles, I remember Omagh, I remember the Shankill Chip Shop bombing, my best friend was killed in the Troubles!'

Jay   You lost a friend?

Ruth   Yeah, she was killed in a bomb in the city centre.

Jay   I'm sorry to hear that.

Leigh   Ruth's actually dedicated the play to her.

Jay   That's beautiful.

Leigh   Gemma Spencer.

Ruth   Yeah. So my mother says ,'You would never have stayed friends with Gemma Spencer anyway. You weren't that close. And she was awful dreary. That whole family was dreary. Her being murdered was the most interesting thing about them'.

I just lost it with her and – I don't know what came over me, I just said, 'Mummy – why do you always have to be such a cold-souled, black-hearted thoughtless fucking bitch?'

Leigh   Oh . . .

Jay   You called your mom a fucking bitch?

Ruth   Uh huh.

Ruth *drinks her wine.*

Leigh   So what happened then?

Ruth   Well, then she crashed the car.

Leigh   She crashed?

Ruth   Yeah

Jay   God . . .

Leigh   Is she OK?

Ruth   No. No she's in hospital. I left her there a few hours ago and got the first flight I could to Heathrow.

She drinks again. **Jay** *and* **Leigh** *are speechless.*

Ruth   It's fine. She's fine. My sister's with her now.

Leigh   Do you need to ring anyone or – ?

Ruth   Yeah, I should. I forgot to pack a charger.

Leigh   Give me your phone.

She hands it to him.

Ruth   Could I get another wine as well?

She knocks back her drink and hands him the empty glass.

Leigh *exits.*

Jay   Wow.

Ruth   Yeah . . . Yeah . . .

Jay   What a journey you've had.

Ruth   Yeah . . .

Jay   I hope your mother's OK.

Ruth   She'll be fine. She's a tough woman.

Jay   You know what they say? (*In a terrible Irish accent.*) '*We do make them tough in the old country.*'

Ruth *laughs nervously.* **Jay** *laughs self-consciously. They sit.*

Ruth   Sorry, I shouldn't have told you all that, I must seem like a real weirdo to you.

Jay   No no.

Ruth   It's because I feel like I know you.

Jay   I feel like I know you.

Ruth   Listen, thank you for doing my play.

Jay   Please! Thank me, thank you! It's the role of a lifetime.

Ruth   I'm your biggest fan. I've loved you since I was like *two*.

Jay   Well, now you're making me feel old.

Ruth   Sorry sorry!

Jay   No, I'm kidding! It means a lot to me that my work has spoken to you.

Ruth   Can I tell you my favourite film of yours?

Jay   Go ahead.

Ruth   Would that be OK?

Jay   Go ahead.

Ruth   *Elixir*.

Jay   Really?

Ruth   That final scene in the car between you and Jack Lemmon?

Jay   *Jaaaack*! I learnt so much from that man. He was like a father to me. When he died I wept for two weeks.

Ruth   Is Jack Lemmon dead?

Jay   I think so. Yeah he is . . . yeah.

Ruth   There's one word for that scene – heartbreaking.

Jay   Heartbreaking is two words.

Ruth   It's one word.

Jay   Hey, you're the writer.

Ruth   I am.

Jay   But I think you're wrong.

Ruth   I'm not.

Jay *smiles.* **Ruth** *smiles back at him.*

Jay   So can I tell you something now?

Ruth   Go ahead.

Jay   Would that be OK?

Ruth   Go ahead.

Jay   Your script. Your fucking script, Ruth. Is the single best script I've read for ten fucking years.

Ruth   That's so nice to hear.

Jay   I mean it.

Ruth   Thank you.

Jay   I hope you don't mind but I sent it to Quentin.

Ruth   You sent it to who?

Jay   Is that OK? I felt I had to share it. It had such a visceral impact on me, it didn't feel right to keep it to myself.

Ruth   Quentin who?

Jay   Tarantino.

Ruth   No way!

Jay   We're talking about doing something together next year and I was telling him about this. He loved it. Is that OK?

Ruth   Of course! Oh my God!

Jay   He said if you were ever in LA he'd love to meet.

Ruth   Are you serious? I fucking love Tarantino.

Jay   Well, he loves you

Ruth   Sorry for swearing but that's too exciting.

Jay   Oh please. I love to swear. I swear like Liza Minelli with a twelve inch cock in her ass.

A shocked, delighted laugh from **Ruth**.

It's cool, I know Liza, she's great. After this is all over, you come out to LA, I'll introduce you to Quentin, we'll get a pizza. How about that?

Ruth   Yes. Definitely!

Leigh *re-enters with a glass of wine.*

Leigh   Ruth, do you need me to call you a doctor or anything?

Ruth   No, I'm fine, he . . . listen to this . . . have you told Leigh?

Jay   No.

Ruth He . . . Jay . . . sent my script to Quentin Tarantino.

Leigh Well, that's . . . wow.

Ruth Oh! I forgot.

Jay What?

Ruth Leigh's not a fan of Tarantino.

Jay *What*??

Leigh No, I think he's great, I just . . .

Jay Are you *insane*?

Leigh No, he's brilliant but I just find the gratuitous violence in his work inherently problematic. It's juvenile. Isn't it? I mean, he's very accomplished but he's not exactly Nuri Bilge Ceylan, is he?

Jay Who is?

Leigh Who is Nuri Bilge Ceylan? I'm glad you asked. Nuri Bilge Ceylan is this extraordinary Turkish *auteur* that I am obsessed with –

Jay Motherfucker, I know who Nuri Bilge Ceylan is! I'm co-producing his American debut.

Leigh Oh. Of course you would know . . . That's wonderful that you're . . .

Jay Nuri would love this play, I really think this play could play anywhere in the world. We need to take this play to Broadway.

Ruth Do you think that's possible?

Leigh You know we've sold out London already? Thanks to this man, we're critic-proof!

Jay Hey, fuck the critics, I don't give a fuck about the critics.

Leigh No, me neither.

Jay   They're fucking animals, Leigh. They're animals, Ruth. And we should do with them what we do with animals. Kill them and eat them. And the good ones keep as pets.

Ruth   I try not to read them.

Leigh   I find it's best to, if you're going to read them at all, you should read them after the run of a show ends.

Jay   Only thing I ever want to read from a theatre critic is a suicide note.

Ruth   Can we actually stop talking about critics? It's making me nervous.

Leigh   You have nothing to worry about.

Jay   Your script is ALIVE.

Leigh   Your words, Ruth, that's why we're here.

Jay   Words words words words words.

Leigh   Language.

Jay   The truth. The truth. The truth. The truth. The truth the truth the truth. The truth. The. Truth. THE TRUTH. The truth.

Leigh   He's right, you know.

Ruth   Well, that's what you have to write, isn't it? The truth.

Leigh   What is there but truth? This is what we go to the theatre for.

Pause. **Leigh** *and* **Ruth** *drink their wine.* **Jay** *watches* **Ruth** *and* **Leigh** *drink.*

Jay   Would you excuse me for a second? I have to make a phone call.

Leigh   Of course.

He puts on a baseball cap.

Jay   Give you both a chance to talk about me.

He puts sunglasses on and flashes a smile.

Jay Cos I *know* that's what you'll do.

Ruth *and* **Jay** *laugh as he exits.*

Ruth Oh my God, he is so – fucking – *real*! He's everything I hoped he would be. Oh my God, I fucking love him.

Leigh Do you want to borrow my phone?

Ruth Why?

Leigh To ring your mother.

Ruth No.

Leigh Or someone in your family?

Ruth It's fine.

Leigh You don't want to check she's OK?

Ruth *No.*

Leigh OK.

Ruth *paces around excited, knocking back her wine.* **Leigh** *has his head in his hands.*

Ruth Do you really think we could go to Broadway?

Leigh With him in it, yeah.

Ruth Do you think Americans would understand the play?

Leigh I don't know. I'm not fucking American, am I?

Ruth What's wrong with you?

Leigh Nothing.

Ruth Are you upset about the Tarantino thing? Look, I'm sorry if you felt I embarrassed you –

Leigh It's fuck all to do with Quentin fucking Tarantino!

Ruth . . . OK . . . so what is it?

Leigh   He said something.

Ruth   What?

Leigh   Something really terrible.

Ruth   What?

Leigh *looks to the door.*

Ruth   Was it about me?

Leigh   No.

Ruth   About the play?

Leigh   No.

Ruth   So why can't you tell me?

Leigh   He said . . .

Leigh *gets up to look out the window, stumbles a bit.*

Ruth   Are you drunk?

Leigh   A bit, yeah.

Ruth   Is he drunk?

Leigh   No, he's in AA. That's all he fucking talks about as well. 'AA! The program! My sponsor!' Has no one in AA told him that the second A stands for anonymous?

Ruth   So what did he say?

Leigh   You won't believe this.

Ruth   Tell me.

Leigh   He said . . . he *said* . . . he wanted to . . .

Ruth   . . . *What*?

Leigh   *Rape. Diana.*

Ruth   Diana?

Leigh *nods.*

Ruth   Diana who?

Leigh   Princess Diana.

Ruth   Are you serious?

Leigh   That's what he said.

Ruth   You're joking?

Leigh   Nope.

Ruth   That's fucked up.

Leigh   I know.

Ruth   Are you sure that's what he said? Because you do have a tendency to exaggerate.

Leigh   I am not exaggerating. Those were his exact words.

Ruth   What was the context?

Leigh   He was talking about some film he made and then he started talking about how if he had to rape a woman, he'd rape Diana, about how it could be good for her.

Ruth   Fucking hell.

Leigh   It was horrendous. It was appalling. I was appalled.

Ruth   So what did you say?

Leigh   What do you mean?

Ruth   Did you tell him you were appalled?

Leigh   I did.

Ruth   And what did he say?

Leigh   Well, then he asked me who I would rape.

Ruth   Who *you'd* rape?

Leigh   Yes!

Ruth   So what did you say?

Leigh   No one. I told him, I told him I found the idea
repellent. Offensive. Misogynistic.

Ruth   Right. And what did he say when you said that?

Leigh . . . He apologised.

Ruth   OK. Good.

Leigh   It was awful. I felt sick when he was talking about it.

Ruth   Well OK . . . so . . . I think it's important right now to
make it clear to him that that kind of comment won't be
acceptable in rehearsals.

Leigh   Well, I think he knows that.

Ruth   But we should be clear with him.

Leigh   But we don't want to offend him.

Ruth   He says something like that to anyone in the theatre
it could jeopardise the whole production.

Leigh   Now you're being hysterical.

Ruth   How am I being hysterical? I'm trying to protect us,
protect my fucking play! I'm doing him a fucking favour
here!

Leigh   Alright! Calm down.

Ruth   Don't tell me to calm down, you're the one being
fucking hysterical, I'm trying to deal with this.

Leigh   OK! Jesus . . .

Ruth   We have to make it clear to him that just because he's
famous he can't be allowed to say and do whatever he wants.

Leigh   But if you say something then he'll know I told you.

Ruth   So what? You already told him you were appalled.

Leigh   Yes, but he also made me promise not to tell
anybody what he said. He was very embarrassed.

Ruth   So why did you tell me?

Leigh   How could I not tell you?

Ruth   Jesus . . . look, I think it's really important for the sake of the play we clarify some professional boundaries. We're all adults here. We can have a conversation.

Leigh   He's not an adult, he's an actor. The best actors, and he is one of the best actors in the world, are like children. Gifted, precious, special children. I understand the psychology of actors much better than you. If you confront him about this, he'll no longer trust me, and then we're all FUCKED! And you'll never get to meet Quentin Tarantino. And I'll never get to run the National.

Noise of **Jay** *entering in the hall.*

Leigh   Please, Ruth! Don't say anything!

Jay *enters.*

Jay   Sorry about that. I was talking to my sponsor.

Leigh   Oh yes?

Jay   I'm part of the program of Alcoholics Anonymous.

Leigh   Yes, I think you might have mentioned that.

Jay   If I'm in a situation where alcohol is present my sponsor likes me to ring him every hour.

Leigh   Oh I'm sorry, we can stop drinking if you like.

Jay   No no, my illness cannot be allowed to affect your behaviour. It's my responsibility to maintain my own sobriety not yours.

Leigh   Well, as long as you're sure.

Leigh *takes a big drink, draining his glass.*

Leigh   Would anyone like another drink?

Jay   Could I have another chamomile tea?

Leigh   Would you like another wine, Ruth?

Ruth   I'll just have a glass of water.

Leigh *exits.* **Jay** *picks up his script and pencil.*

Jay   Do you mind if I . . . ?

Ruth   Not at all.

Jay   Interrogate?

Ruth   Go ahead.

Jay   So first question:

Ruth   Yes?

Jay   What is Ulster?

Ruth   What is Ulster?

Jay   I mean I understand what it is, it's a *place*, right?

Ruth   It is a place, yes.

Jay   But I need to know specifically.

Ruth   Well, Ulster is historically part of Ireland.

Jay   History is so important to this. For this play, I feel like I need to know the history of Ireland like I know my own ball sack.

Ruth   OK. Ulster is another name for Northern Ireland. It's what loyalists like Tommy usually call Northern Ireland.

Jay *writes this down.*

Jay   Great. Second question – do you think I could have an eyepatch?

Ruth   An eyepatch?

Jay   I think it would be a great metaphor for my character's moral decay.

Ruth   I don't see a reason for it.

Jay It's a metaphor.

Ruth OK.

Jay So that's a yes?

Ruth No. I was just saying 'OK'.

Jay I took that as a yes.

Ruth Well it wasn't.

Jay OK . . . OK . . .

He flicks through his script.

Jay So, on page thirty-three, this line puzzles me . . .

Ruth Which one?

Jay When Tommy says he's British.

Ruth Uh-huh?

Jay Why does he say he's British?

Ruth He says he's British because he is British.

Jay But why would an Irishman call himself British?

Ruth Because he's a unionist. Unionists call themselves British. Like me. I'm a unionist. I'm British.

Jay You're British?

Ruth Yes.

Jay But you're Irish?

Ruth No.

Jay No what?

Ruth No, I'm not Irish. I'm British.

Jay OK . . . So that's interesting. So you're British because you're what? You're British because . . . now let me try to understand this . . . you're British because . . . No, I'm sorry, I don't get that?

Ruth   Well –

Leigh *enters with drinks.*

Leigh   Here we are.

Jay   Leigh, you told me Ruth was Irish.

Leigh   She is Irish.

Jay   But she says she's British.

Ruth   I am British.

Leigh   Yes well OK, I know that's a thing you say, Ruth, I know you call yourself British, and you're in some ways part-British. Perhaps in historical terms British.

Jay   History is so important to this.

Leigh   Oh, it's vital.

Jay   I was just saying this. I have to know the history, the cultural woodwork of this play, like I know the contours of my own genitalia.

Leigh   Mmmmm

Jay   So historically Ruth is British?

Leigh   Sort of, yes.

Jay   Even though she's Irish?

Ruth   I'm not Irish.

Leigh   She is Irish.

Ruth   I'm not Irish. I'm British.

Jay   Are you British because Britain used to own Ireland? So they used to own you, like a slave, so you're British?

Leigh   Exactly!

Ruth   They never *owned* me. I was never a slave!

Jay   It's confusing because to me you sound Irish.

Ruth   I sound Northern Irish.

Jay   Northern Irish is still Irish though, right?

Leigh   Northern Irish is still Irish, yes.

Jay   Because 'northern Irish' sounds to me like *Irish* but from the *northern* part of Ireland?

Leigh   That's right.

Ruth   But Northern Ireland's part of the UK. The UK is British. I was born in the UK. So I'm British.

Jay   OK, I think I'm starting to understand.

Leigh   It's very complicated, the whole history of the region is very complex and tragic that's why Ruth's voice is so important in helping us understand this tragic and complex history. Particularly in this disastrous post-Brexit nightmare we're living through.

Jay   Is Brexit relevant to this?

Ruth   Not really.

Leigh   Completely. Brexit was a tragedy for Northern Ireland, it undermined the Good Friday Agreement, the peace process.

Ruth   To call it a *tragedy* is a bit melodramatic.

Jay   Could there be a return to war?

Ruth   I don't think so.

Leigh   It is possible though. That's why the play is so important.

Ruth   A *play* isn't going to reverse Brexit.

Leigh   Not on its own, but as part of a general cultural resistance.

Jay   So if Tommy is British?

Ruth   Yes?

Jay   Why does he hate the British?

Ruth   He doesn't.

Leigh   But he does, doesn't he? He has that speech about betrayal.

Ruth   But that speech is about the failure of successive British governments to defend the British people of Ulster. Tommy feels betrayed by the British state, there's a difference.

Leigh   Is there? Most English people I know are indifferent to Ulster unionism, if not downright hostile, embarrassed by what they see as a meaningless hangover of colonialism.

Ruth   I don't understand your point, Leigh.

Leigh   My point is that Ulster unionists aspire to be British when most real British people want nothing whatsoever to do with them.

Ruth   We don't aspire to be British. We are British. We don't need your permission to be what we are.

Leigh   Well . . .

Ruth   What?

Leigh   You sort of do need our permission to be British, don't you?

Ruth   You don't get to decide who's British and who isn't.

Leigh   Well, we sort of do. That's the point. That's what the Empire was all about. Which is why imperialism was such a shameful chapter in our history.

Jay   History. It all comes down to history.

Leigh   Everything is history. Because history is everything.

Jay   This is more complicated than I thought.

Leigh   Don't worry we have four weeks.

Jay   So my character is British?

Leigh   Not really.

Ruth   Yes.

Jay   He thinks he's British?

Leigh   Yes.

Ruth   Because he is British.

Jay   But he hates the Fenians. He wants to kill them all. 'The Fenians.' Right from the first speech.

He reads in a terrible Belfast accent.

'Dirty fucking Fenian bastards. Dirty fucking Fenian cunts. Fenian fucking cuntbags.'

He looks up.

Jay   So?

Ruth   So what?

Jay   Well, that's the British he's talking about. The Fenians are the British. Right?

Pause

Leigh   Nnnnoooo. That's not right . . . Ruth?

Ruth   No, Fenians are . . . uh . . . The Fenians are not the British, no.

Leigh   The Fenians are the Catholics. Right, Ruth?

Jay   Catholics?

Ruth   Yeah. Well, Irish Republicans or nationalists, Catholics.

Leigh   It's an offensive term used by Protestants.

Jay   Offensive?

Ruth   Can be, yes.

Leigh   It's a bit like the n word isn't it, Ruth?

Ruth   No. It doesn't have the same kind of history.

Leigh   History. That word again.

Jay   So the word Fenian is offensive to Catholics?

Ruth   It depends on the context. When Tommy uses it, it signifies hate, anger, murderous rage.

Jay   So it's hate speech? You admit you've written hate speech?

Leigh   Well, it's a play. It's a dramatic construction. Ruth isn't motivated by hate.

Jay   And when Tommy celebrates 'killing Fenians', when he talks about driving all the Fenians out of Ulster, 'murdering all the Fenians', he's talking about killing Irish Catholics?

Ruth   Yes. That's the point of the speech.

Leigh   But that's not Ruth's point, is it? That's Tommy's point?

Jay   He's talking about killing innocent people? Because they're Catholic?

Ruth   Yes.

Jay   But I'm Catholic. I'm Irish Catholic.

Ruth   OK.

Jay   He's talking about killing people like me. Are we endorsing the murder of innocent people here?

Leigh   But it's a character. Right, Ruth? You as a playwright are not condoning murder, are you?

Ruth   I think my feelings are quite complicated about this. And I think the play is complicated about this subject. I think in the context of Northern Ireland it's hard to say that the murder of innocent people was always wrong. The UVF did murder many innocent people, innocent Catholics.

Which was a deliberate strategy to terrorise the nationalist population. To weaken support for the IRA. Who were also engaged in a campaign of sectarian murder. Now, the British government, the British army, had no vested interest in protecting working-class Protestant communities from IRA attack. We were completely vulnerable. And while the UVF undoubtedly behaved monstrously . . . they murdered the innocent, they murdered children, in the case of the Shankill Butchers, they hacked limbs from bodies, they decapitated so called 'innocent Catholics', disembowelled them, as Tommy does in the play. But if they weren't there, what would the IRA have done to us? They were our last line of defence – the Protestant community's only line of defence – against one of the world's most well organised, well-funded ruthless terrorist machines. Funded, I might add, in large part, by wealthy Irish Americans like yourself, Jay. So . . .

Leigh   So . . . what Ruth's saying here is she is dissecting murder. She is dispassionately examining the historical circumstances that allow ordinary people to commit extraordinary acts of violence. Isn't that right, Ruth?

Ruth   I'm not sure that is what I'm saying.

Jay   Wait, wait, wait. Wait.

They wait.

Is she a Protestant?

Ruth   Yes. Is that a problem?

Jay   Well . . .

Ruth   *Is* it a problem?

Jay   Yeah, I . . . I kinda feel like I've been lied to here.

Ruth   By who? By me?

Jay   By both of you.

Leigh   In what way?

Jay   I feel that I was approached with this project on the understanding it was a story about the struggle for Irish freedom, written by an Irish Catholic. And now I find it's a story about the murder of Irish Catholics written by a British Protestant, written by someone I would consider a traitor to the cause of Ireland.

Ruth   Excuse me?

Leigh   Jay, no one at any point said anything about Ruth being a Catholic or a Protestant. I didn't realise it was important to you. And secondly, I know she says she's British but she's Irish.

Ruth   I'm British.

Leigh   I know you perceive yourself to be British, but in terms of how the rest of the world perceives you, you're Irish.

Ruth   I don't care what the rest of the world thinks.

Leigh   And that's great. That's why you're such a ferocious, uncompromising, indispensable artist. But the fact of the matter is that most audiences who see this play, theatregoers in London by and large will see you as an Irish writer and will receive this as an Irish play. The notion that the Ulster Protestant community is in any way British is absurd to most real British people. They won't understand that any more than you will, Jay. This is, I promise you, really not an issue.

Jay   I have to take some time to consider if this is really a project I want to be involved in.

Ruth   What?

Leigh   Well, wait just a second here. We start rehearsals tomorrow.

Jay   I know that.

Leigh   There's a contract here.

Jay   There's a contract here.

He points to his heart.

Here! OK?

Leigh   OK.

Jay   I have a contract with a power greater than myself!
OK?

Leigh   OK.

Jay   And I have a contract with my Irish ancestors! OK?

Leigh   OK. I hear that. I respect that. But you do have an
actual legal contract with us.

Ruth   Have you ever been to Ireland?

Jay   Me?

Ruth   Yeah have you been to Ireland?

Jay   The north or the south?

Ruth   Either.

Jay   No, I haven't been to either.

Ruth   Jay. I'm a British citizen. Where I come from, union
flags are flown with pride from every rooftop. There are
symbols of Britishness everywhere – the crown, the Red
Hand of Ulster, the King James Bible. I grew up watching
British TV, studying British history. I went to a British
university, I've built my career and reputation in Britain.
And generations of my family have given their lives in wars
for Britain. And you? You've never even been to Ireland. So
why is it absurd for me to call myself British? But it's not
absurd for you to call yourself Irish?

Leigh   Who are you asking?

Ruth   Anyone who'll answer me.

Leigh   It's a good question. I don't know the answer.

Jay   My blood is Irish.

Ruth   My blood is British.

Leigh   This is excellent. No, it is. This discussion is really helpful for the play. This is what Marx would term praxis. Just imagine what Brecht would make of this conversation!

Jay   But, you see, in my mind, now. In *my* mind. This is over. This is over now. You have to find someone else.

Ruth   Can he even do that?

Leigh   Well now, this is a, we're all very nervous, we all feel like this the night before rehearsals, but you're doing the fucking play, I mean come on. You're doing the fucking play, Jay!

Jay   I was led believe this was an Irish play by an Irish writer.

Leigh   It is an Irish play. She is an Irish writer!

Ruth   It's a British play and I'm a British writer.

Leigh   Oh fuck off, Ruth!

Ruth   What?

Leigh   That is so disingenuous. Part of the reason people take you seriously as a writer is because you're writing about Ireland, Irish history. You wouldn't be taken so seriously if you came from the fucking Home Counties. I have built my reputation on discovering Irish writers and directing Irish plays. I know an Irish play when I see one, Jay. This play is about a psychopathic terrorist released from prison under the terms of the Good Friday Agreement who roams the backstreets of Belfast decapitating Catholic priests because he believes the ghost of Bobby Sands is trying to send him to Hell. It couldn't be more Irish if it tried. It's as Irish as a fucking potato famine.

Jay   I've made up my mind. I'm out.

Ruth   Fine. We'll get someone else.

Leigh   Well let's not . . . come on now . . . There must be some kind of compromise we can reach here.

Jay   I don't see how.

Leigh   Are there changes Ruth can make to the play?

Ruth   I'm not changing anything.

Leigh   Keep an open mind. Please, Ruth.

He thinks.

Jay   Make Tommy a Catholic.

Ruth   No.

Leigh   Wait, Ruth.

Jay   Put him in the IRA.

Ruth   No fucking way.

Jay   And there's gotta be dancing.

Ruth   Dancing?

Jay   Irish dancing.

Leigh   Like Riverdance?

Jay   People love Irish dancing. And if we want to go to Broadway, this play needs to be Irish.

Leigh   It is Irish.

Jay   More Irish. It needs to be as Irish as a pig fucking his sister in a peatbog. Let's get a pig! A live pig! Think about it!

Leigh   Well, I'm not sure about the pig but Irish dancing is very theatrical. It can be effective.

Ruth   Protestants don't dance.

Leigh   Well that's . . .

Ruth   It's true.

Jay   Everyone dances.

Ruth   Protestants don't.

Leigh   That's all the more reason to put it in. Challenge stereotypes.

Ruth   I thought you both loved the truth of the script.

Leigh   We do.

Ruth   Its authenticity.

Jay   I can't fault its authenticity.

Leigh   But you know, if anything it's almost too authentic.

Jay   That's a really interesting thought. Go with that.

Ruth   What are you saying?

Leigh   I believe its authenticity is potentially alienating.

Jay   Yes! That's . . . he's . . . yes!

Ruth   Why have you never mentioned this before, Leigh?

Leigh   I always felt there was some kind of problem.

Jay   I did too. I couldn't put my finger on it but –

Leigh   If this play has a weakness and I don't believe it does but if it has a weakness, it's its –

Jay   I think I know what you're gonna say.

Leigh   It may be a guilty of certain parochialism.

Jay   Parochial, yeah. That's what I –

Leigh   A certain introspective uh

Jay   Mentality.

Leigh   Mentality, yeah, a mindset.

Jay   A mindset, yeah.

Leigh   That's something the critics might, they could pick up on.

Jay   They definitely will.

Ruth   I thought you didn't care about critics.

Jay   I don't. But you do.

Ruth   You told me this was the greatest script you'd read for ten years.

Jay   That still holds true.

Ruth   And Leigh, when you first read it you compared it to Pinter.

Leigh   I stand by that. In many ways it's better than Pinter. I think if Pinter were still alive he'd admit that himself.

Jay   It reminds me of Chekhov. When I read this, I thought, I have to do this. This chick is the new Chekhov.

Ruth   *Chick?*

Leigh   Well, don't be . . .

Ruth   Don't be what?

Leigh   He's saying something complimentary. Honestly, Ruth, a great actor compares you to Chekhov and all you focus on is chick!

Jay   I'm sorry for saying chick. It was purely for alliteration.

Ruth   I'm not making Tommy a Catholic. I'm not making him a member of the IRA. That's not happening.

Jay   . . . OK . . .

Leigh   What if he wasn't a Catholic. But also he wasn't a Protestant.

Ruth   What?

Jay   Go on.

Leigh   This story is so universal you could really set it anywhere. You could set it in Doncaster or Wolverhampton, or Chicago or Cape Town.

Ruth   I'm not rewriting the play so it's set in Wolverfuckinghampton.

Leigh   And I'm not saying you should.

Ruth   I don't even know where Wolverhampton is.

Leigh   Well, maybe you'd know where Wolverhampton was if you were –

Ruth   What?

Leigh   Genuinely British.

Ruth   I'm not changing a word of this play.

Leigh   You're not listening to me, you're letting your bloody –

Jay   Emotions.

Leigh   Emotions – thank you, Jay – you're letting your bloody emotions get in the cloud. I mean cloud your –

Jay   Judgement.

Leigh   Judgement, thank you, Jay. It's like your mother said, Ruth – nobody wants to hear about the Troubles anymore.

Ruth   Don't mention my mother.

Leigh   But with just a few cuts, it can become a universal –

Ruth   I am not cutting a fucking word. I'm not cutting a fucking word from this –

Leigh   If you'll listen to me –

Ruth   I AM NOT CUTTING A FUCKING WORD FROM THIS PLAY. Fuck you and fuck you. I am not cutting *A WORD*.

Jay   Whoah.

Leigh   Look.

Jay   I am not used to being spoken to like this, Ruth. I like your balls. If you were a man I'd put your balls in my mouth right now. And I'm not even gay.

Leigh   Look. You've been in a car crash.

Ruth   That's completely irrelevant.

Leigh   Your mother's in hospital.

Ruth   Stop talking about my mother!

Leigh   But I think it's affecting –

Ruth   Stop talking about my fucking mother!

Leigh   Ruth.

Jay   Ruth.

Leigh   Ruth.

Jay   Please Leigh, let me. Ruth. I understand. I do. I also am an artist. Directors are not – no offence, Leigh.

Leigh   No, none taken.

Jay   But directors are not artists in the same way that writers and actors –

Leigh   I completely agree. I myself see myself as a *liberator* of artists, an enabler.

Jay   I know Leigh is right here. My instincts are never wrong. This play could play anywhere in the world.

Leigh   The *world*, Ruth.

Jay   If you let us explore and and

Leigh   Reimagine it.

Jay   Reimagine it, exactly. Also.

Leigh   Yes?

Jay   It allows us the opportunity to revisit the question of the eyepatch

Leigh   Oh.

Jay   Because an eyepatch is universal. Everywhere in the world, everyone knows what an eyepatch is.

Leigh   That's true.

Jay   Any audience in the world could see an eyepatch and think . . . 'That's an eyepatch'.

Ruth   Look. We all know what's going on here.

Leigh   What's going on?

Jay   What's going on?

Leigh   What is going on?

Jay   I don't understand.

Leigh   What's going on here is we're trying to put on a fucking – bring some fucking ground-breaking art into the world. And it's what the world needs.

Jay   'Zactly. Now more than ever.

Leigh   This disastrous environment of the post-Brexit disaster.

Ruth   You're letting him get away with this because he's a movie star. You wouldn't put up with this from Simon Russell Beale.

Leigh   I'm insulted by that. No, I am.

Jay   I think we both are. You're being insulting, Ruth.

Leigh   And the worst of it is you're insulting Simon. I'm trying to do what's best for the play. And this glorious genius of an actor– I'd cast him if he were a complete unknown.

Jay   Thank you. And I know that's true.

Ruth   Even though he can't do the accent?

Jay   What?

Leigh   *What?*

Jay   I can't do the accent?

Leigh   Your accent is perfect.

Jay   I've worked really hard on the accent. (*In the accent.*) *'How now brown cow.'*

Leigh   It's perfect.

Jay   *'You're telling me I don't sound like an Irish fella.'*

Ruth   It's really bad.

Leigh   I strongly disagree.

Ruth   You sound like a Belfast Dick Van Dyke. Like you're Dick Van Morrison.

Jay *gets up.*

Ruth   As long as we're talking about truth here . . .

Leigh   Jay, please don't leave.

But he's not leaving. He goes to his bag. He takes out his Academy Award. He places it on the table. **Jay** *looks at* **Ruth**. **Ruth** *looks back at him.* **Leigh** *looks at the Academy Award.*

Jay   You want to talk about the truth. This is my truth. I take it with me everywhere I go. To remind myself that I mean something to the world. That my work resonates with people. That I will not be to spoken to as if I am a piece of shit. When someone treats me like a piece of shit and it never happens but when they do I bring it out. I display my truth. And my truth is speaking to you right now, Ruth. It has something to say. It's saying I'm right. I'm right about your play. And even if I weren't right its presence here makes me right. Change the play. Perhaps if you do, you too may find yourself the owner of the truth one day too. There are no coincidences. The universe, God, Vishnu, Medea, is speaking to you now. And if that doesn't mean something to you then nothing means anything.

Leigh   Nothing means anything, exactly.

Jay   Make this a story for everyone.

Leigh   Yep.

Jay   A story a Jew or a Muslim, a fucking Welshman or a kid in Alabama.

Leigh   A suffering Palestinian.

Jay   Some kid with no shoes in a shanty town in Cairo.

Leigh   A, a, a, kid from the Bronx whose brother's just been shot by a racist police officer.

Jay   A teenager in some European city like Prague who's thinking to himself 'You know what? I might be a fucking woman'.

Leigh   Or a, a, Congolese immigrant in the suburbs of Paris who's considering suicide –

Jay   could come and see your play and say – This is My Story too. All it needs is . . .

Leigh   Yes!

Jay   Yes!

Silence. They watch **Ruth**. *She looks the Academy Award. Then looks at* **Jay**.

Ruth   Would you like to rape me?

Or do you only rape dead princesses?

Silence.

Leigh   . . . OK . . .

Jay *stands up. He goes to exit.* **Leigh** *chases after him and blocks his exit.*

Leigh   Jay Jay, please don't leave!

Jay No, I don't have to be here right now. I don't have to be treated like this.

Leigh I am well aware of that.

Jay I don't have to be in England arguing about a fucking play!

Leigh I understand how you're feeling, Jay, I do.

Jay I turned down James Cameron to be here!

Leigh Completely, I know.

Jay Why did she say that?

Leigh I've no idea.

Jay Is she insane? What kind of person says a thing like that?

Leigh I'll get her to apologise. Ruth apologise.

Ruth No I don't think so.

Leigh Apologise, Ruth! He doesn't have to be here. Didn't you hear him? He turned down James Cameron to be here!

Ruth Fuck James Cameron.

Jay *Excuse* me? Did you just say fuck James Cameron? Did she just say fuck James Cameron?

Leigh I know, but bear in mind her mother's in hospital.

Jay I don't know how to talk to this person. I can't be part of a dialogue with someone who questions the artistic legacy of Mister James Cameron. I'm done here, Leigh.

He goes to the door and turns back.

I happen to know a little something about American cinema and James Cameron is the greatest filmmaker in the history of our art form and more than that he is a pioneer, a philanthropist, an inventor of worlds and a benefactor. He's the American David Lean. He's the American Tarkovsky. He's the American Bergman. How can you deny that?

Ruth   He's Canadian.

Jay   I'm outta here.

He starts to go but **Leigh** *stops him.*

Leigh   Wait!

Jay   I'm leaving.

Leigh   Let me talk to her. Come on. Let's not end things like this. I'm sure we can still find a way through. Remember what brought you here. The play is still the play. You are the only actor for this role. And as for your Belfast accent, to my ears it's perfect. And most of the audience who come to see this will be from my socio-economic background. It's unlikely anyone from Belfast will ever hear about this play.

And Ruth, Jay's right. You are the new Chekhov. You're better than Chekhov. You're Chekhov with jokes. Real jokes, not Russian jokes.

We were both so excited when you said yes to this part. The only actor of his generation comparable to Brando and Clift. *Montgomery* Clift. And *Marlon* Brando . . . (obviously) . . .

Celebrity does unusual things to people like us. It does, Ruth. We expect too much of our celebrities. And the bigger the celebrity the more we expect. And the bigger our disappointment when they fail to meet our ridiculous expectations.

We've talked a great deal tonight about honesty and truth. So let me be honest.

Before Ruth arrived tonight you made a comment, which discomfited me. I felt compelled to share this comment with Ruth when she arrived.

Specifically it was your comment about Princess Diana.

I found this comment deeply distressing. The comment yes, but also who made this comment. An artist, in my view, *sans pareil*. I was disappointed. And I relayed my disappointment to Ruth when she arrived. I now see that I shouldn't have. I realise now, having got to know you better, that this comment was intended ironically. It was a thought experiment. We've asked you to come here to engage with this thematically very troubling play. We can't then ask you to not access subconsciously your own dark side in preparation. We start tomorrow morning after all. Whether you knew it or not, you were getting under the skin of the character, enveloping yourself in this play's psychically devastating undercurrents.

Ruth wanted to confront you about your comment. And I stopped her. That was wrong.

A great man once said that workers in the theatre were the 'engineers of the human soul'. Well, the human soul is a messy and unforgiving country. And our currency in this country is honesty. If we are unable to give voice to the erroneous thought, the unspeakable comment then our currency will lose all value. And so will the human soul. The human race depends upon us, the makers of theatre, for its very survival. And without the freedom to be wrong in the pursuit of the truth, then we're no better than actual engineers. We're no better than theatre critics.

Jay   You told her what I said?

Leigh   I did.

Jay   I said those things in confidence.

Leigh   It was an unforgiveable betrayal. But I hope we can move past it.

Jay   If it's unforgiveable how can we move past it?

Leigh   That's a very good question.

Jay   I trusted you.

Leigh   And I trust Ruth. She won't repeat this conversation to anyone. Will you, Ruth?

They look to her.

Ruth   Why did you say it?

Jay   It was hypothetical. I was saying who I would choose to
. . . if I had to . . .

Ruth   Rape?

Jay *nods.*

Ruth   So say rape.

Jay   . . . Rape.

Ruth   So you chose . . .?

Jay *nods.*

Ruth   Say her name.

Jay   Diana.

Ruth   I don't understand why you would say something like
that in the first place.

Jay   Because I was saying she could have turned it around,
made it into a positive experience.

Ruth   Why Diana?

Jay   Because of how she – Who she was – and the good
work she – this is what I'm saying – this movie I was in – it
was in context of this –

Ruth   You see, I think it's disgusting.

Jay   Disgusting?

Ruth   You're disgusting. That you would think that, let
alone say it. That you would not just contemplate raping a
woman but you would speculate about who exactly that
would be. What kind of sick mind comes up with something
like that?

Leigh   Ruth, I know it seems –

Ruth   And you chose Diana because she's what? Powerful? Totemic? Iconic? Because she was better than you? You want to put her in her place, is that it?

Jay   No. I love strong women. I chose her bec –

Ruth   You want to bring her down to size. Remind her she's nothing compared to your dick? Your big powerful dick? I bet it's fucking tiny.

Jay   Not true!

Ruth   I bet it's fucking microscopic.

Jay   Now look. You're crossing a line here. There's a line. And you're crossing it.

Ruth   Have you ever raped anyone?

Jay   Jesus . . .

Ruth   Have you?

Jay   I'm embarrassed you would even ask me that.

Ruth   I wonder. Everything I've seen from you tonight makes me wonder. What have you done? Who are you really?

Jay   Are you accusing me of rape? Because of a . . . a thought! You listening to this, Leigh? She's calling me a rapist. Where's your evidence?

Leigh   Just be careful what you're saying, Ruth.

Ruth   I don't know if you're a rapist.

Jay   OK then.

Ruth   But I do know you're a fucking prick.

Jay   That's it. We're done here.

Leigh   Let's just –

Jay   No fuck her! Fuck her, Leigh! She needs to apologise. For everything she's just said.

Ruth   I have nothing to apologise for.

Jay   I can't believe this is happening! I am one of the nicest people in this business. Ask anyone! I love women. I respect all women. My first manager was a woman. A black woman! Of colour! I respect you, Ruth, as a woman and as an artist, but if you don't apologise to me right now, I will make it my life's work to destroy you like the cunt you are.

Ruth   Excuse me please.

Ruth *disappears into the kitchen.*

Jay   I can't tolerate this, Leigh. I can't be in her play. Not after what she's said.

Leigh   I understand how you're feeling.

Jay   She's going to have to apologise.

Leigh   I agree. I think this has all gone too far.

Jay   Too fucking far, yes!

Leigh   I think we should all apologise.

Jay   Who?

Leigh   All three of us. I think we've all said things tonight we shouldn't have.

Jay   I'm not apologising. What the hell do I have to apologise for?

Leigh   Well . . .

Jay   She's the one being unreasonable here.

Leigh   You just called her a cunt.

Jay   That was intended as constructive criticism.

Ruth *returns with her phone.*

Ruth   Hey, Jay!

He turns.

Ruth   Say cheese, motherfucker!

She quickly snaps a photo of him.

Ruth   OK, Jay, you're going to be in my play and there'll be no cuts. You'll say every word I've written. And you won't wear a fucking eyepatch.

Jay   Why would I agree to that?

Ruth   Because I've composed a tweet and I'm ready to hit send. 'Tonight Jay Conway told me he wanted to rape Princess Diana.' You stay and do the play, or I'll tell the world what you said.

Jay   Gimme the phone.

Ruth   Stay away from me.

Jay   Leigh, get the phone off her.

Leigh   Don't do this, Ruth.

Jay steps towards her.

Ruth   Stay the fuck away or I hit send!

Jay   Do not send that tweet. Delete it. Delete what you've typed. Delete the tweet.

Ruth   OK, Jay . . . here's what I want . . . I want you go back to your apartment now. I want you to start learning your lines and work on your Belfast accent until it's at least passable. We'll see you tomorrow morning at ten o'clock sharp. Over the next four weeks you're going to work like fuck, you're gonna work like a Paddy on the railway, and you're gonna give the Tony-award-winning performance of your fucking career. And then you and I are gonna fly out to LA together first class where you'll introduce me to Quentin Tarantino and any other motherfucker in Hollywood I want to meet. And then. *Then*. I'll promise not to send the tweet. And everything that's gone on here tonight will stay between the three of us.

Deal?

He goes towards her.

Ruth   Stay away.

He stops. Then goes again.

Stay the fuck away.

Leigh   OK, look.

Jay   I need that phone, Leigh. She can't expect me to tolerate this.

Leigh   I'll get it off her.

Ruth   No you won't.

Jay   She's a very disturbed young woman. She's disturbed and damaged and she has to be stopped.

Ruth   You both stay away from me.

Jay *paces around, tortured.*

Jay   Fuck! FUCK FUCK FUCK!

Leigh   Let's all stay calm.

Jay   I will not be held to ransom by a fucking tweet!

Ruth's *phone rings. They all watch her. She stares at the number.*

Leigh   Are you going to answer it?

Ruth   Keep him away from me.

She answers it.

(*On phone.*) Hello?

OK . . .

OK . . .

Can I call you back in five minutes? I'm just in a meeting.

Thanks for letting me know. I'll call you back.

She hangs up.

Leigh   Ruth?

Ruth   Yes?

Leigh   Why don't you give me the phone? I can take care of the phone while we work out some kind of compromise. Ruth?

Ruth   Yes?

Leigh   Are you listening to me?

Ruth   No.

Leigh   Well could you listen to me, please? We're in something of a fucking crisis situation here I think you'll agree.

Ruth   My mother's dead.

Leigh   Oh.

Oh.

Well, I'm . . . I'm very sorry to hear that. Uhm . . . I think . . . I think the three of us should all . . . you should go back to your apartment Jay, and Ruth, if you like, you can sleep in the spare room. I'm assuming you'll want to get back to Belfast in the morning? Ruth?

Ruth *nods.*

Leigh   I'll get the theatre to book you the first flight we can.

Ruth   I'd appreciate that, thanks.

Leigh   As regards the production, let's uh . . . let's just all get a good night's sleep. A lot's happened tonight we all need to process. In the morning, I'll ring both your agents and we'll work out what to do next. I think we've all got a bit carried away and forgotten about the bigger picture. There are more important things in life than putting on a play.

Ruth *is lost in her thoughts, in a state of shock.* **Leigh** *watches her, perhaps tries to comfort her.* **Jay** *tries to get* **Leigh**'s *attention.*

Jay (*whispering urgently*)   Leigh . . .

Leigh *looks at him.* **Jay** *performs a mime of flying, tweeting birds to represent 'Twitter'.* **Leigh** *looks confused.* **Jay** *does an 'X' mime.* **Leigh** *looks more confused.* **Jay** *then mimes 'tweeting on a phone'.*

Leigh (*whispering*)   What are you . . .?

Jay *beckons* **Leigh** *to come over.* **Leigh** *checks in with* **Ruth** *who is still lost in shock/grief/confusion. Then he joins* **Jay**, *both of them still whispering and checking* **Ruth** *isn't listening.*

Leigh   What?

Jay   The tweet.

Leigh   The . . .?

Jay *does his bird mime again.*

Leigh   Ohhhhhh . . .! So why were you doing that?

Leigh *does the 'X' mime.*

Jay   X.

Leigh   What?

Jay   X. That's the new name for Twitter!

Leigh   Is it?

Jay   Yes!

Leigh   Since when?

Jay   I dunno, since . . . who gives a fuck?

Leigh   So, what's the problem then?

Jay   Well, I need some kind of reassurance she's not going to send the tweet. The X.

Leigh   I don't think we need to worry about that right now, do we? Her mother's just died.

Jay   I'd feel better if you had her phone.

Leigh *goes back to* **Ruth**.

Leigh   Ruth. Would you mind if took your phone?

Ruth *doesn't respond. She's lost in her thoughts.* **Leigh** *sneaks up to her. He gently takes the phone from out of her hand. She doesn't notice.* **Leigh** *and* **Jay** *watch.* **Leigh** *gives* **Jay** *a surreptitious glance. He nods at* **Jay**.

Ruth   Can I use your bathroom?

Leigh   Of course.

They watch her disappear into the bathroom. **Jay** *goes immediately to* **Leigh**.

Leigh   Her phone's locked.

Jay   We need her passcode.

Leigh *fiddles with the phone.*

Jay   This is fucked. This whole situation is fucked. If she blackmails me I will sue you. I'll sue your fucking theatre.

Leigh   Relax! It will not come to that! Hopefully now that her mother's died she'll have a different perspective on all this. Proves your point actually.

Jay   What point?

Leigh   About Diana. That good things can come from terrible events.

Jay   And why the fuck did you tell her what I said about Diana? You're such a little *bitch*!

Leigh   Well, there's no need to call me a *bitch*!

Jay   You betrayed me, motherfucker!

Leigh   I know. And I'm sorry. But Ruth is one of my dearest friends. I thought I could trust her.

Ruth *re-enters unseen by them.*

Jay   I could have told her what you said about Thatcher. Let's not forget that.

Leigh   Well, hold on here, what I said was not in the same league as what you said.

Jay   What you said was much worse.

Leigh   No it wasn't.

Jay   You said you wanted to punish Margaret Thatcher by raping her.

Leigh   I never said that.

Jay   I was trying to help Diana. Make the world a better place.

Leigh   OK. OK. Thank you for not telling her.

Jay   Whole situation is fucked.

Leigh   We're not fucked. You still want to do the play, don't you?

Jay   Not like this. I came to do an Irish play. Not Protestant propaganda!

Leigh   Well, the great thing about her mother being dead is she'll be away for at least a week and even when she does come back her mind won't be on the play. We can really shape it into whatever we want to. We can cut what we want.

Jay   You don't think she'll object?

Leigh   Not once she sees how much better we'll make it. I understand Ruth's process – she's sensitive, fragile, haphazard. She writes from her *id*, it's wild and free and poetic – but there comes a point where she needs rational guidance. Most women writers are the same. As are most Irish writers. She's Irish and a woman so she needs it more than most.

Ruth   No.

Leigh   Oh. Ruth. We were just talking about –

Ruth   You're not cutting anything.

Leigh   How long have you been . . .? Of course we wouldn't cut anything without your permission.

Ruth   You're cutting nothing, Leigh. You're cutting nothing.

Leigh   How are you feeling?

Ruth   How am I feeling?

Leigh   Yeah how do you feel?

Ruth   I feel I'd miss my mother's funeral before I'd leave you two untrustworthy cunts alone with my play.

Leigh   OK.

Ruth   But that's so typical of me, isn't it? I'm so sensitive and fragile and haphazard. I'm so Irish!

Leigh   I'm sorry you heard that but I meant all of it as a compliment.

Ruth   So you want to rape Margaret Thatcher?

Leigh   No.

Ruth   To punish her?

Jay   Context.

Ruth   What?

Jay   There was a context.

Ruth   What was the context?

Leigh   Well, he was . . . there was a gun to my head.

Jay   Rutger Hauer had a gun to his head.

Leigh   It was Jesus actually.

Jay   Jesus had a gun to his head and asked him who he would –

Ruth   Rape, I know. But you told me you refused to answer.

Leigh   I did, didn't I? Initially.

Jay   He did, yes.

Ruth   You told him he was a misogynist.

Jay   I don't remember that. You think I'm a misogynist?

Leigh   I didn't use those exact words.

Ruth   Why Thatcher?

Leigh   I was worried Jay would be offended if I didn't come up with an answer and so I thought of the worst woman I could think of and . . .

Jay   I wouldn't have been offended. You thought I would have been offended?

Leigh   Well, when I did refuse to answer, you were offended.

Jay   I wasn't.

Leigh   You were. You were acting all weird.

Jay   No I wasn't.

Ruth   So you lied to me?

Leigh   You did act weird, you went very quiet and intense.

Jay   That's part of my process. I can't believe you thought I was offended.

Ruth   Look at me, Leigh.

Jay   I'm offended now. *Now* I'm offended.

Ruth   You lied to me?

Leigh   Yes. I was worried you wouldn't understand. And I was right. You don't understand.

Ruth   I understand exactly what's happened here.

Leigh   You're not appreciating the context.

Ruth   But you lied. You said you didn't answer but you did answer. And now you're planning to betray me by changing my whole fucking play while my   mother is . . . fucking . . . while my mother . . . my mother . . .

Leigh   Ruth, please.

He goes to her.

Ruth   *Fuck you!*

Jay   Ruth, just –

Ruth   *And fuck you*!

Leigh   I did it for you!

Ruth   For me?!

Leigh   Yes!

Ruth   For fucking *me*?!

Leigh   Everything I've done tonight has been for you. For your play! To get your play on! To keep him happy! Including saying I would rape Margaret Thatcher. You know me! You know I'm not capable of that! I'm the biggest fucking feminist you'll ever meet! No one has done more for women in theatre than I have. Look at you!

Ruth   What about me?

Leigh   Well, you wouldn't have a fucking career if it wasn't for me! I believed in you when everyone thought you were shit. I kept your career alive! So yes, for the sake of the play, for your sake, because I care too much I said I would rape Maggie Thatcher. I'm fucking sorry! But I also said that as awful as she was, as horrendous and evil a human being as that woman was, even she didn't deserve to be raped. Because no woman deserves to be raped.

Jay   He did say that.

Leigh   Despite the fact she herself was practically the worst rapist this country's ever seen, that she raped the miners, she raped the trade union movement, she raped the working people of this country, despite all that even she doesn't deserve to be raped.

Ruth   So if you disagree with a woman it's OK to rape her?

Leigh   That is not what I'm saying and you know it. Don't twist my words.

Ruth   It sounds very like that's what you're saying.

Leigh   I'm saying that she didn't deserve it. That no woman deserves it, even a woman as evil and cold and inhumane as Thatcher! As a socialist you surely understand where I'm coming from?

Ruth   Who said I was a socialist?

Leigh   As a social democrat.

Ruth   Who said I was a social democrat?

Leigh   As a person on the left.

Ruth   I'm not on the left.

Leigh   What do you mean?

Ruth   I'm a conservative.

Leigh   What?

Ruth   I voted Conservative in the last election.

Leigh   Fuck off.

Ruth   And in the local elections.

Leigh   I don't believe you. You're saying this to hurt me.

Ruth   I intend to vote Conservative in the next election too.

Leigh   Next you'll be telling me you voted for Brexit.

Ruth   I did vote for Brexit.

Leigh   Oh God.

Jay   Are you OK?

Leigh   I know you only said that to hurt my feelings. I get it. I've hurt you. I've betrayed you. Now you're pretending to betray me.

Ruth   I don't see how I've betrayed you.

Leigh   But how could anyone *sane* vote Brexit?

Ruth   I don't like the European Union. I don't see how that has any bearing on our friendship.

Leigh   This is a betrayal of everything we've worked towards. You cannot be a Brexit-voting Tory bastard! I refuse to believe this! You're a fucking artist!

Ruth   So artists are only allowed to think one way?

Leigh   What's thinking got to do with it? It's not about thinking! It's about feeling! It's about empathy! It's about foodbanks! And fucking austerity and fucking . . . foodbanks! Tell me you're not a Tory. As a woman, as a feminist . . . You're not even British! You're fucking Irish! You shouldn't even have a vote on Brexit! You can't tell anyone.

Ruth   I can't tell anyone what you said?

Leigh   Well, you can't tell anyone what I said but you also can't tell anyone you voted for Brexit. Nobody will ever commission you again.

Ruth   I've no intention of telling anyone.

Leigh   It would ruin your career. Your career would be over.

Ruth   Like me telling everyone you're a misogynist.

Leigh   Why would you call me a misogynist?

Ruth   You joke about raping women.

Leigh   It wasn't a joke.

Ruth   So you were serious about raping women?

Leigh   No, fuck off, Ruth, you know I'm not a misogynist. I adore women. I want to be a woman. I wish I was fucking trans! That's how much of a feminist I am.

Ruth   Give me my phone.

Leigh   Why?

Ruth   Give it to me.

Leigh   Why do you want your phone?

Ruth   Because it's my phone.

Leigh   You're not going to tweet are you?

Ruth   That's my business.

Jay   Don't give it to her.

Ruth   Hand me the phone now.

Leigh   I need assurances that you're not going to put anything on social media about me.

Jay   Same.

Leigh   On Twitter.

About what I said.

Ruth   I need to ring my sister.

They look at her. **Leigh** *doesn't know what to do.*

Ruth   My mother has just died. I want to speak to my sister. I need my phone.

Leigh *looks at* **Jay**. **Jay** *shakes his head disapprovingly.* **Leigh** *hands* **Ruth** *the phone.*

Ruth   Thank you.

She appears to be texting on her phone.

Leigh   What are you doing? Ruth?

Ruth   I'm texting her.

Leigh   You said you were ringing her.

Ruth   I'm texting her to ask if it's a good time to talk.

She keeps texting.

Jay   She's tweeting.

Leigh   What?

Ruth   I'm not.

Jay   She's on Twitter. She's tweeting.

Ruth *speeds up her typing, walks away from them.*

Leigh   How do you know?

Jay   I can see in the mirror.

Ruth *speeds up her typing, tries to run as they grab her and try to get the phone out of her hand.*

Ruth   Fuck off!

Leigh   Give me the phone!

Ruth   Get the fuck away from me!

Jay *bites* **Ruth**'s *hand. She screams in pain. Blood pours out of her hand.*

Jay   Get the phone! Delete the tweet!

Leigh *picks up the phone. He fiddles with it, trying to delete the tweet.* **Ruth** *goes for him but* **Jay** *physically restrains her.*

Leigh   I'm not a Twitter user. I don't know how to operate the app!

Jay   Show me!

Leigh *holds up the phone,* **Jay** *looks at it. While he's distracted,* **Ruth** *stamps on* **Jay**'s *foot. She escapes from his grasp. She grabs*

Jay's *Academy Award and smashes it over his head two or three times. He stumbles and falls. She goes to* **Leigh**.

Ruth   Give me the phone.

Leigh   Now wait –

She smashes the Academy Award over **Leigh**'s *head. She beats him with it until he stops moving. She goes to get her phone as* **Jay** *struggles to his feet. As* **Ruth** *almost gets the phone,* **Jay** *grabs her by the throat, pushing himself against her, choking her. She gasps for breath. She is on her knees.* **Jay** *stands above her, choking her. She reaches on the ground and finds* **Jay**'s *pencil on the floor. She drives the pencil deep into* **Jay**'s *eye. He screams in agony, as blood pours out of him.* **Ruth** *stands up, covered in blood, the Academy Award still in her hand.*

Ruth   Now you can wear a fucking eyepatch!

Leigh *moans in pain. She steps over him and grabs her phone out of his hand. She types her tweet and presses send. She sits exhausted, phone in one hand, Academy Award in the other. Lights slowly down as her phone buzzes and beeps with notifications.*

Printed in the USA
CPSIA information can be obtained
at www.ICGtesting.com
LVHW020901171024
794056LV00002B/661